The Boy Who Wanted to Change the World

Moments From a Life in Search of the Positive

The Autobiography
By Shad Helmstetter, Ph.D

The Boy Who Wanted to
Change the World

Published by Park Avenue Press
362 Gulf Breeze Pkwy., #104
Gulf Breeze, FL 32561

Helmstetter, Shad
    The Boy Who Wanted to Change the World

ISBN-13: 978-0-9836312-6-2 *Printed format*
ISBN-13: 978-0-9836312-7-9 *Digital format*

For more information on the author and his work, visit
www.shadhelmstetter.com.

Table of Contents

Introduction

Imagine what you would do if you could change the world. What would you do if you were possessed with that one idea—that you could actually make a difference—and that idea never went away?

Beginning when I was very young, there was something I imagined. I had a serious dream; I imagined I could change the world. I believed I could do something that would help people change their lives. This was not a vague, now-and-then dream; it was a vision that defined my childhood and my youth, and it went on to set the direction of my life.

I am writing this autobiography because, after searching many years for a way that I could help to make a positive difference in people's lives, I found what I was looking for.

The answer was the discovery of a concept that would end up changing many people's lives, and it led to the writing of a number of books, the first of which was *What to Say When You Talk to Your Self,* first published in 1986. After 45 successive printings, it was updated with a new edition in 2017. That book is about how we become "programmed" from birth on, and how we live our lives controlled by those programs—bad or good.

The discovery, which I introduced as the concept of "self-talk," is the role that our own words and thoughts play in our programming and our success or failure in life—and how science has shown that each of us can actually rewire our brain with positive new programs. The discovery was that we can change our programs—and with that, we can change our lives.

That discovery was a turning point in my life. After the book *What to Say When You Talk to Your Self* was published, I was invited to appear on every popular radio and television show of the time–

–with repeat appearances on Oprah Winfrey, CNN News, ABC, CBS, NBC, and on hundreds more radio and television shows and interviews.

Meanwhile, I was also appearing in television infomercials, talking about self-talk, and the concept was being introduced to millions of television viewers through those infomercials. Then, while I continued to write books and appear on additional television and radio programs, I also began speaking in person to audiences, many times to thousands of attendees, throughout the United States and then in other countries around the world.

But even with all that, my journey was just beginning. If I wanted to make a difference, and actually contribute something that would help the world become a better place, it would not happen overnight, or even in a few years; I would have to make the choice to dedicate my future to bringing my dream to life. This included writing more than twenty books, founding two training institutions, and speaking to thousands of audiences over more than three decades.

Autobiographies come in different styles. Some of them tell each detail of the story of the life of the author chronologically, step by step. Others hit only the highlights. And still others focus on the moments that the author feels were the most important to fulfilling the purpose of that person's life. Mine is in the third category. This autobiography is a look into the experiences that I believe most directly impacted my path through life, and where that path has taken me.

The previous books I've written fit into the category of self-help, but this autobiography is different. It is a collection of snapshots of my life, what influenced me, and what I learned from each of the experiences I write about. But even though this is not written as a self-help book, I hope that some of the ideas that have helped me along the way may, in some way, also help you.

Because this autobiography is not a time-line of my life, written for purposes of historical record, I have taken the liberty of presenting each of the moments within it where it seemed to me to fit the best, and that is what determined the order of the chapters.

You'll find in the stories and moments from my life that there is a thread which runs through them. That thread reinforces my belief that there is a direction to life; that life's varied stories, when viewed together like beads on a string, seem not to be accidents, but rather parts of an underlying script, like the theme of a movie, and we do our best when we choose to participate in the writing and directing of our own life scripts. It is better to get in sync with the universal force that drives us, instead of fighting it or ignoring that it's there.

Now, after I have spent a good number of years on this journey, I'm writing this autobiography to share with you what I have learned. As you read through the following chapters, I'll share with you what set me on my path, and also some of the moments of my awakenings, my discoveries, my challenges, my failures and my successes.

Along the way, after each chapter, I will tell you what I learned from the experience I've just shared. I hope some of these moments will be an inspiration to anyone who feels, as I do, that each of us is here for a purpose, and that if you want to make a difference, you *can*.

Chapter One
A Few Finger Snaps in Time

When I recount stories and key moments from my life, in my own mind it can seem like the time has flown by. But I was prepared for time to pass rapidly; I was forewarned. I actually first learned about the fleeting nature of time, and how important time is, when I was just six years old, and it is one of the first experiences I had that I recognized later as having influenced my life.

It was on my sixth birthday that I had my first real birthday party. Among the relatives and friends who had been invited was a very special older man. His name was Eli, a distant uncle of mine.

I liked Eli because he was very wise, and he knew something about everything. But I liked him most because he was my friend, and he would always take the time to talk to me, and to explain new things to me.

It was sometime during that sixth birthday party that old Uncle Eli told me he wanted to talk to me. So we went outside and sat down on the wooden bench under the pine trees in front of my home. It was night, and the sky was filled with a million, dazzling stars.

"How old are you now?" Eli asked as we sat there.

"I'm six years old," I said, very proudly.

"Can you snap your fingers?" Eli asked next.

"Sure I can," I answered, knowing that any six-year-old kid ought to be able to snap his fingers.

And with that I snapped my fingers, once, really loud, just to prove it.

"That's very good," Eli said. "Now, there is something very important I would like you to do for me."

"Sure, if I can," I said.

"Exactly one year from now, next year at this time," Eli went on, "I want you to go outside, sometime during your seventh birthday party, when you're another year older, and look up at the stars. Then I want you to remember the moment we're sitting here right now, and snap your fingers, just once. Will you do that for me?"

Even though I didn't know what Eli was telling me, or why, he was a very wise uncle, and I was happy to agree, so I promised.

"If I'm able to be at your party next year, I'll go outside with you when you snap your fingers," he said.

Then he continued, "And this is just as important. I'd like you to snap your fingers again, another year later, on your eighth birthday, and then again on your ninth birthday, and then on your tenth birthday."

Eli paused to make sure I was understanding him, and when I nodded my head "yes," he continued.

"And then, I want you to snap your fingers again on your fifteenth birthday, and then again on your twentieth birthday, and then on your twenty-fifth, and on every *fifth* birthday after that for as long as you live. Every five years, sometime during your birthday party, take a few minutes and go outside by yourself, and look up at the stars, think about tonight, and snap your fingers, just once. Will you do that for me?" he asked.

I promised Eli that I would, even though I still couldn't figure out why he was asking me to do that. But I knew he was very smart, and he was my friend, so I promised.

Then Eli said, "Let me hear you snap your fingers again."

So once again, I proudly snapped my fingers, as loudly as I could.

5

"That's good," Eli said. And then he added, "By the way, did you notice that between the time you snapped your fingers just now, and when you snapped your fingers the first time, a few minutes ago, *it seemed like no time at all passed* between those two times you snapped your fingers?"

I partly understood what Eli meant, but not completely. In fact, it wasn't until a year later, when I was seven, that it finally became clear to me. Old Uncle Eli couldn't come to my birthday party that year. He had gone to sleep one night during the summer, and never woke up again. He had passed away quietly in his sleep.

But I remembered the promise I had made to him. So during my seventh birthday party, I went outside by myself, and sat on the same wooden bench old Eli and I had sat on a year earlier, under the pine trees, and I looked up at the night sky that was filled with a million stars. And I thought of Eli, and I snapped my fingers just once.

It was in that *moment* that I realized the amazing secret Eli had given me: *It seemed as though not a single moment had passed between the first time I had snapped my fingers—a year earlier—and the time I snapped my fingers just now.* In a single finger snap of time, *an entire year* had gone by!

And so I snapped my fingers again on my eighth birthday, and again on my ninth birthday and again on my tenth.

And then, as I promised Eli I would, I snapped my fingers on my fifteenth birthday, and again on my twentieth and on my twenty-fifth, and on my thirtieth—and every fifth birthday thereafter. On each of those occasions, sometime during my party, the celebration of my birth, I would excuse myself for a few minutes, go outside by myself, and wherever I was, I would look up at the stars, think of that first time, and snap my fingers just once.

Some time ago, I celebrated my sixty-fifth birthday. And as I stood out under the stars that night, and snapped my fingers just once, I thought about all the years that had passed between that first finger-snap so many years ago, and now, and I realized that I had journeyed from the boy—to the middle-aged man—to the older man—in just a few, brief finger snaps in time.

Soon I will snap my fingers under those stars again . . . and then again on another birthday . . . and then on another . . . for as long as I am here. And each time I do, I will think again about the secret that old Eli taught me: that *it is what we do between the finger snaps that counts.*

On one occasion, when I was grown, I was alone on my birthday, and I was hoping my son Anthony would call. He, too, was grown, and had a family of his own. But it was my birthday, and I hoped he would remember.

The evening got later and later, and I was beginning to wonder if I would have much of a birthday at all. I was about to give up hope, when finally the telephone rang. I picked up the receiver and said, "Hello," expecting to hear my son's voice on the other end of the line. But there was nothing but silence.

I said "*Hello,*" again—but I still heard nothing.

And then, finally, I heard it, loud and clear, and in that moment my spirits lifted to the sky. What I heard was the clear and unmistakable sound of a *finger-snap!*

It was my son, sending a message to me across the miles, across the memories, and across the years, reminding me he had not forgotten.

Not long after, on my grandson Anthony Junior's sixth birthday, my son took his young son Anthony outside to talk with him alone. And while father and son sat there together, under the stars, and talked about life, and about being six years old, my son said to my grandson, "How old are you?"

"I'm six years old," little Anthony said, very proudly.

7

And then my son looked up at the stars and smiled, remembering, and said to his own son, "There's something I'd like you to do for me. *I'd like you to snap your fingers, just once.*"

In the journey from boyhood, and wanting to change the world, to now, this is my story. This is some of what happened between the finger snaps of my life.

What I learned:

From the finger snap experience with old Eli, I learned that it's a good idea to listen to wise, older people who have something important to say.

I also learned the key point Eli was trying to teach me—that our perspective of the time we have to live our lives is an illusion, and that real life passes faster than we think. That early lesson from Eli taught me to get things done, to move forward, and not wait, because in another finger snap, the time to do it may have passed.

But in addition to that, the finger snap lesson first suggested to me that time itself, as we know it, may not actually exist. As I will relate in a later chapter, this idea became so strong in my mind, that it changed my view of time itself, and I would one day have to fight to defend that position. But that is a story for later.

Chapter Two
Battle of Wits

It's possible that most people who make it into middle age believe that their own childhood was unique, or different in some way from everyone else's. I feel that way myself.

But I won't dwell on the notion that my own path was formed by having a childhood that was blessedly different. I'll just say that when I've looked around, I haven't yet found any other home that was anything quite like the home I grew up in. And without any doubt, it was that home and that family and that environment which played the designing role in creating the life and the path I followed.

I was raised on the outer edge of a small Midwestern farm town. To the back of our home, behind our yard and across an alley, was the small town we lived in. It was a town that was only about a mile square. To the front of our home, across a cinder street, there was nothing but a small grove of plum trees, and then endless farmland.

My family consisted of my two parents and six children—three girls and three boys. All eight of us lived in a home that was a little over 600 square feet. It had only three small rooms—one that was both kitchen and living room, and two bedrooms, each only big enough for a bed and a small closet. Many living rooms are bigger than that entire house.

After a few years of trying to pack everyone into that small house, my father moved a bare plywood work shack on wheels to one of the doorways, and attached it to the house; that would be my parents' new bedroom. I remember going into that freezing cold bedroom on winter mornings, and seeing small, little snowdrifts on the floor that had sifted in through spaces in the plywood walls overnight.

Other people thought we were poor, but I had no idea that was the case. Until I looked back on it years later, I didn't even recognize that my family had lived drastically below the poverty level my entire childhood and youth. But while many people remember a lot of times of unhappiness or hurt in their childhood, my memories, without hiding any of them, were mostly happy ones.

What we had in abundance was an incredible will to overcome odds, and an unending spirit of creativity. There never seemed to be a moment when someone wasn't creating something. My father's frequent advice to "throw the book away" was based on his lifelong conviction that you could always find a better way to do something. If someone else had already done it, find a better way.

That philosophy formed the foundation of a family culture which caused the six children in my family to see everything as an opportunity to improve things, reinvent things, and solve problems in inventive new ways.

And my father was always at the head of this brigade. He was so incredibly inventive that we were never surprised at anything he did. He made things, built vehicles, welded things together, and constructed things, and they always ended up working. (He made a farm tractor—a field sprayer—from an old car frame and engine. It was the only farm tractor in the county that could do 70 miles an hour driving down the highway.) He handmade our first bicycle—a unisex model for both the boys and the girls—and it was faster and sturdier than any other bike in town. He lowered a large, two-truck garage down onto a brand-new concrete block foundation (that he had built under it) by placing giant blocks of ice all around the top of the entire concrete foundation and allowing the garage to settle into perfect position when the blocks of ice melted—and slowly lowered the garage into place on the new foundation. He was a genius. He taught us that you could solve any problem if you were willing to look at it in a completely new way.

My father's inventiveness was a perfect role model for all of the kids in our family, and each of us grew up in an environment that was rich with discovery and ideas. We were always encouraged to research things until we found the right answers. If we had a question, we had a family encyclopedia, and we looked it up. Anything creative we did was rewarded with acceptance, making creativity an expected thing instead of an exceptional thing.

The natural sibling rivalries that brewed among us were almost always formed around someone knowing something that someone else didn't know, and the result of this was that we always had to be on our toes to stay up on anything new—science, math, philosophy, anything at all.

What brought all this together was that we had an absolute rule that the family always ate supper (our evening meal) together, every day, with almost no exceptions. My father had built an extra-long picnic table with long sitting benches on each side to accommodate all eight of us, and that was our dining room table at which we ate every supper together. (Because our house was too small to have a dining room, the picnic table we ate at was in the kitchen.)

The "everyone eats together" rule was brilliant. It created an extended time every day where everyone in the family got to talk, listen, share ideas, ask questions, and learn. There was no subject that could not be shared or talked about at that table. Any idea, no matter how small or how big, could be talked about. I don't remember a single time when we were told that an idea that one of us had, no matter how impossible, was stupid or foolish. So instead of living in an environment that destroys dreams, my family was creating an environment where dreams are listened to, and where dreams begin their life.

Part of what made this possible was that our parents also strictly enforced a "no arguments" rule, so we had to learn to give and take without fighting or getting angry; we had to learn to be peaceful even if we disagreed. We learned humanity, caring about others, by learning to care for each of the people who shared that table every day.

Our mother was, as many mothers seem to be, a saint. During the day, when sibling rivalries did get out of hand, she was referee and peacekeeper, and eternally gentle and measured. She also worked tirelessly, endlessly. Just keeping track of six kids would have been enough, but managing the household while she trained first one kid and then the next in how to help with all the chores—cleaning, cooking, washing clothes—was a job that was more difficult then, because our home didn't have any of the usual appliances and conveniences that most homes had. (We had a hand crank washing machine, no regular bathroom, no bathtub or shower, and finally got hot running water only later in my childhood.) But our mother managed it, and never once complained. On Saturday evenings, after supper, my mother would play beautiful music on her violin, and neighbors a block away would sit outside on their porches, so they could listen.

My father decided to never have a television in our home, and we never had one. That choice proved to be one of the greatest blessings to my childhood. Instead of sitting and watching television, we had to be creative. None of us liked being bored, so that meant we had to be constantly thinking up things to keep us occupied.

One of the early things we did as kids was to create a game that was so fascinating and entertaining that we played it a lot in the evenings after supper, and we continued to play this game throughout all the years of my childhood and youth. We named

12

the game "Battle of Wits," and it was an exceptionally interesting game because it had *no rules*, and it had no set goal, other than that one team would win.

That could lead to just about anything. We would choose two teams, and one team would hide their eyes while the other team left. If you were on the waiting team, you didn't know where the other team went or what they were doing or what their goal was. So you had to discover that, and if you could figure out what it was, you had to try to outsmart the other team and do it better. Sometimes the other team would just hide; sometimes they might create a code you had to guess; sometimes they would all be in trees, seeing who could climb the highest; and sometimes they would be making something.

Sounds confusing, I know, but if you played the game for years, you became very inventive and resourceful. We often played the game until long after dark, so late into the evenings that we would hear the town whistle that blew mournfully every night at ten o'clock, and the grass was getting wet with dew, and we had to leave the game and go inside and go to bed, and wait to play the game again the next night. The name of the game describes it perfectly: Battle of Wits was about being creative—about thinking smart.

I believe that it was a family culture of respect for thinking smart—building intelligence and appreciating knowledge—as well as an environment of active learning in our home that created this unendingly interesting kids' game. I don't recall at any time witnessing one of my brothers or sisters *"acting smart"* or acting as though they thought they were better or smarter than someone else. There was never any conceit. *Thinking*, and thinking *well*, was just part of a home life that everyone accepted as natural.

Adding to the respect for thinking and knowledge was an unusual level of interest in creativity—expressed by all of the kids in the family. One by one, each of the children in the family began to express himself or herself creatively in some way. Our parents didn't openly encourage us to become writers or artists or designers or natural inventors; they just seemed to accept that "creative" is just how children are.

I recall, as an example of our notion of creativity, a discussion I had with my mother when I was about seven. My mother had told me that I should not have taken a large metal soup spoon outside and used it to dig in the dirt, because as she said, soup spoons were for eating soup—not digging in the dirt.

But I thought my mother was wrong, and I did my best to explain that we only "think" a spoon is for eating soup, when it can be used for anything that its shape suggested we could use it for—digging, mashing, measuring, scraping, stirring, reflecting images upside down, catapulting stones or marbles, or, with two of them, playing them like a musical instrument or drumming on a Quaker Oats box like a drum—and that the *least* of a spoon's uses was for actually eating soup. (All true, but I still lost the argument.)

All of us children went beyond having an average interest in creativity, and in later years, that creativity in many forms became major areas of activity for each of us.

Each of my three sisters is an accomplished artist in oils and other media; one of them became a professional fashion designer; another, a writer and a sculptor; another plays piano, cello and viola, and my remaining brother is a remarkable artist who creates furniture and beautiful things out of wood. He also became beautifully proficient on the violin, learning to play it for the first time when he was in his sixties.

I believe that the high level of creative output among all of us siblings during my childhood and youth was fostered and enhanced by the natural joy of finding purpose in creativity, along with the sibling group acceptance and approval that was so central to our home life.

Because we lived in a *very* small home, with little space for privacy, any creative idea one kid was working on was available for everyone to see and comment on or discuss. That, coupled with sitting together during supper every night, and talking around our kitchen picnic table, cemented a one-family community that worked together, played together, and learned together.

Each of us also developed a deep and lasting appreciation for music. In addition to our mother's beautiful violin playing on Saturday evenings, nearly every evening before he went to bed, our father put a stack of classical music records on the record player, leaned back in his easy chair, closed his eyes, and for the next hour, listened to music and invented things in his mind. Anything he was going to build or construct later, he would first work out completely and in detail in his mind. So while he was mentally "inventing" each evening, we were listening to classical music playing.

To this day, every member of our family loves and appreciates classical music of all types. Even now, when I'm relaxing and Debussy's *Claire De Lune* or Beethoven's *Moonlight Sonata* is playing in the background, I see my father, now long since passed away, sitting in his easy chair, eyes closed, thinking deeply, imagining and creating something wonderful in his mind.

What I learned:

When I ask myself where my own life in search of the positive, my love of knowledge, and my endless interest in the mysteries of life came from, it is clear that a few short—but important—scenes from the movie of my own childhood tell the story. My love of humanity, creativity, beauty, structure, and endless expression came from a supper table made from a wooden picnic table with benches that sat in our small kitchen, and gave each of us a chance to listen, a chance to talk, a chance to learn, and a chance to dream.

When I left that home, one of the lasting things that I took with me most, along with the love and support of the family that surrounded me, was the inspiration of the game of Battle of Wits. It was the lesson of that childhood and youthful game that taught me to always be willing to look at any problem in a whole new way. It embodied a simple philosophy that shaped my life.

As a result, from childhood on, "creativity" would become one of my greatest friends in life—reminding me to always be willing to think in a creative way about anything. Which opened the door to everything.

Chapter Three
Treasure

There is an incident from my early life that contains both a mystery—one that, amazingly, has never been solved—and also a message that, to this day, continues to influence my thinking. It is the true story of a childhood "treasure" in my own life.

When we see the world as children see it, there is a spirit of adventure in all of us. We are born with it. And sometimes in our lives, usually when we are still young, if we're lucky, that spirit of adventure comes to life. And if we're really lucky, we go for the adventure, and in doing that, we have an experience we will never forget.

For me, the unforgettable experience was the search for a treasure. Even at the time it happened, perhaps part of me knew that, as a young person, any idea of searching for a real treasure was something that only happened in the movies. But this one was real. It was a life experience of a kind that would not only stay with me, but also be a lesson that would influence my view of life.

Here's what happened:

Across the small street from our home was an old, deserted house, one we thought for certain was haunted. Almost hidden by thickets and sheds and stands of old trees, it was the kind of place you would avoid on a dark moonless night when broken screen doors creaked on their hinges and branches tapped at dark, staring windows.

Even on the brightest day, that old house, with its abandoned woodsheds and its unruly landscape of weeds and tall dark trees, conjured up visions of hidden secrets and buried treasures from

17

the past. For highly imaginative kids, the old house and its surrounding tangle of landscape represented unending possibilities.

It didn't always occur to us that we might only be imagining most of what we believed about the old place. So we weren't at all surprised when, one day, an old man arrived on that haunted old property and began to rummage through the dilapidated buildings as though he was searching for something.

He was a gaunt scarecrow of a man, thin and bony, with sharply articulated features and dark, piercing eyes. He was not a kind man, or friendly. He didn't like kids, and he especially didn't like us when we approached him and asked if we could help.

The first day, when we saw him pulling loose boards from old woodshed walls and digging in the dirt floors of the old outbuildings, we tried to talk with him, to learn what he was doing. But instead of talking to us, he gruffly turned aside, and went about his business of looking and digging and prodding and searching.

Since we were adventurous kids, it did not take us long to figure out that this old man actually *was* searching for something—and we suspected it just might be the treasure we had imagined finding all along. So we had a "kids only" meeting and decided that we should do everything possible to learn as much as we could about the treasure we were sure he was searching for.

The old man never did warm up to us. But he did end up letting us help. He agreed to give each of us a nickel if we found something that looked like a "box." And that's all he would tell us.

Earlier, on one of our more daring forays into the interior of the haunted old house itself, we had found a yellowed scroll of paper, written in a language we could not read, hidden in the wall of an upstairs room.

On another occasion, we were hiding in the ditch on our side of the street from the old house, and we watched a stray black Labrador retriever, barking at something. He was standing in front

18

of the old cellar doors that angled downward, low to the ground, from the side of the house, and he was looking intently at the cellar doors and barking, and he wouldn't stop. The cellar doors were closed over the stone steps that led down into the cellar beneath the house.

We were astonished when we watched the cellar doors open, as if opening by themselves, just far enough to let the dog enter, which he did, and then the cellar doors closed again, and the barking stopped.

My sister Holly said she recognized that dog; it belonged to the optometrist who had an office in our town. So we ran into our house and Holly called the optometrist to ask if his dog was missing, and it was. The optometrist immediately drove out and met us on the street by the old house. We told him we had seen his dog go into the cellar and then the cellar doors had closed behind him. We didn't know who had opened the cellar doors to let the dog enter, and we were too scared that it was a ghost or something to go over there and open the doors ourselves.

But the optometrist wasn't afraid; he made his way through the weeds, over to the cellar doors, reached down and pulled one of the doors open . . . and there was his dog, sitting on one of the stone steps that led down into the cellar. The dog couldn't go into the cellar itself. The reason was that the entire cellar was flooded with water, all the way up to the step where the dog was sitting. There was no one and nothing else there but the dog and the water!

After that episode, it was impossible to convince any of the kids who had been there and seen it happen that there weren't ghosts in that old house.

But now, with an old man searching for something, we had a new mystery on our hands. We had learned from questioning our parents that the old man, in his seventies or eighties, was a member of a family that had emigrated from Europe, and was the brother-in-law of the person who had built the old house many years earlier. We had also been told that we should avoid the old man, and that we should not play on the property where he was spending his time each day.

The old man searched a long time, but the only thing he ever found was an old, faded, purplish, leather sack that contained three rusty old keys. This he had found behind the wallboards of one of the old sheds. Finally he left, taking the three keys with him, and we never saw him on the property again.

But what fire his presence had added to our imagination! Now we *knew* that the old house *did* have a secret. The old man had given us more belief in our treasure than we could ever have created for ourselves. Now we were *sure* that the treasure existed. And now we could find it for ourselves.

And so we set out. We were not exactly the sort of group you would expect to find any treasure at all: My older sister, Holly, who was thirteen, my seven-year-old brother Verne, a twelve-year-old neighbor girl, and me, also twelve, made up the crew.

We had known from exploring the property that there was a very unusual grouping of large smooth stones lying in a small stand of trees. In that group of trees, half buried in the dirt and leaves, was a large stone the size of a man's body. Just above the body stone was one round stone, like a head. There were also two straight, long stones extending down from the bottom of the body stone, like two legs, and one more long stone, like an arm, extending out from the side of the body stone. Together, the five stones created the perfect image of a man lying on the ground, head, torso, and legs, and one arm pointing very clearly in one direction. Those stones, we thought, were the clue. Their arrangement might be giving us the direction to the treasure.

If you plotted a straight line from the extended arm of the stone man, it pointed directly toward the center of three solitary trees that stood in the shape of a perfect triangle about twenty feet from the stone figure. *That point,* we reasoned, in the exact center of those three trees, right where the stone arm was pointing, must be where the treasure was buried.

At this time in my life, as adventurous as my friends and I were, we had one mighty adversary. Once we had found the spot where we knew the treasure might be, we had to overcome only one obstacle—my father.

He had told us that *none* of us, *for any reason,* could play on the property that surrounded the old house. Unfortunately, the area our father had placed off limits was also the location of our buried treasure. If we were to dig it up and live a life of riches—which we now totally believed we would—not only would we have to disobey a direct order from our father, we would also have to avoid getting caught digging a large hole on the property where we weren't supposed to be in the first place.

Our solution, as it so often was in cases like looking for treasure, was to do it anyway. In this instance, one of us would stand guard, a lookout in the event the evil pirate—Father— showed up unexpectedly, and the rest of us would take turns digging.

We started early the next Saturday morning. We marked the spot, and we dug. I turned the first spade, and then with each shovelful began to dig with an increasing sense of urgency. What if, I thought, someone, especially our father, found out what we were doing? He wouldn't understand. And so we dug rapidly, and the first few shovelfuls soon turned into a clearly defined excavation, three feet across and five feet in length.

The ground under the three trees had stones in it, and we had to stop often to pull the larger stones out of the way. At a depth of about three feet, we ran into a large root from one of the trees, and after some coaxing we convinced the neighbor girl who was with us to run home and get an ax or a saw so we could cut the root. If any of the rest of us went to our own home, it might tip someone off, and at the time, she was the best candidate for the least notice.

It was almost noon when I found myself standing in a hole about four feet deep in the ground, digging out scoops of black soil, when the shovel struck something hard. It wasn't a rock and it wasn't a root. I started to dig faster, and every shovelful I threw out of the hole confirmed the reality of my wildest dream. I doubt that any experience I had ever had up until then could have compared to the excitement I felt at that moment.

We had found it! Revealed to me, and to the others gathered anxiously around that incredibly important hole we had dug in that forbidden ground, was the top of a chest. It was hard, it was solid, it was old, and it was *real*.

The old man had been right! We had been right. There *was* a treasure—and we had found it! Buried in the ground was a chest. I handed my shovel to one of my teammates, and I remember dropping to my knees to scrape away the last of the soil that covered the top of the chest. It was magnificent! It was an old curved-top chest with riveted metal bands shaping its top. I couldn't believe it was really happening. I began to dig with my hands, scraping and scooping the dirt from around the chest, looking for the clasp or the lock that held it shut.

And suddenly, there it was. I brushed the dirt from the lock so those standing above me could see it. The lock was old and rusted, and it was packed with the soil it had rested in for what must have been many years of hiding. And in the face of the lock were three large keyholes.

I shouted for someone to give me something to break open the lock, but then eyeing my shovel, I grabbed it and began to attack the lock as though it were guarding the greatest treasures of the universe.

It was then that my sister Holly sounded the alarm. Through my excitement at finding the chest, I still remember her urgent shout telling us that we had been spotted and our father was on his way, headed in our direction. Of any news I could have heard at that moment, that was the worst. To be where we weren't supposed to be was bad enough. To be caught digging a big hole in the ground was worse. But for anyone at the age of twelve or thirteen, letting an adult find out that we were uncovering a treasure would have been *unthinkable*.

With a menacing adult about to discover our secret, we did the only thing we *could* do. We hurriedly began to shovel dirt back into the hole. At the time, it didn't matter if we had discovered the richest cache of gold and jewels that had ever been found; for the moment, getting rid of the evidence was the only thing that mattered.

By the time my father arrived on the scene, all he saw was a three-by-five-foot hole in the ground, about two or three feet deep. Someone, I forget who, blurted out the first words of an instant and incredible story—that we were digging a goldfish pond. He didn't buy it, but he couldn't figure out what we were really doing either, so he did the only parent-like thing he could do. He stood there and watched over us as we refilled the entire hole. Then he told us that some suitable punishment would be doled out later, and he made us promise that we would never dig on that property again. We promised that we never would.

I have forgotten what punishment was meted out. I suppose, at the time, my head was too full of the possibilities of what that chest contained to worry too much about having to do a few extra chores or being banished to my room and going to bed that night without supper. And so the chest, and whatever it contained, was buried again and was once again left to rest, safe from the few inspired kids who had nearly unlocked its secrets, hidden from the rest of the world that no longer remembered its existence.

To this day, not one of the original crew of treasure seekers, now all adults, has gone back to find out what was buried in that hole. It wasn't that we were told not to—as adults, any of us could have gone back at one time or another to find it again, but we never did.

All of the treasure hunters have long since moved away from our home town. For those of us who had almost touched the dream, the story of the treasure is now a tale we tell to our children and to our grandchildren.

Some years ago, I visited that small town where an old wooden chest lies buried in the ground in the center of three tall trees. I flew from my home in another state, rented a car at the airport, found my way to the blacktop roads of the open countryside, and headed off into the afternoon sunshine. It was a day much like the summer day many years earlier when my friends and I had had our great adventure.

When I arrived in the peaceful little town, I drove along the street I had walked so many times to and from school, until I came to the place where my childhood home had once been.

The small house I had grown up in wasn't there anymore; a new, larger home had taken its place. The cinder road had become a nicely blacktopped street. The grove of plum trees was gone. It had been replaced by a row of apartments. The old haunted house, too, was gone or had been rebuilt; a newer-looking home stood in its place. The land around it had been cleared, and the woodsheds and tall dark trees had given way to a well-kept garden surrounded by a wooden fence.

But I could not help noticing that in one particular part of the neatly trimmed lawn, there were three tall trees in the shape of a perfect triangle that had survived. I parked my rental car and got out to say hello to the man who was cutting the grass under those trees. The five large stones that looked like a human body were gone, and in their place was a small white gazebo. It looked like the sort of place where the man and his wife could sit and enjoy the evenings. I did not tell the man who was cutting the grass

24

beneath the three tall trees, that about four or five feet beneath the ground he was walking over, was an old chest with a rusted three-key lock.

After talking to the man for a few minutes, telling him that I used to live in a house across the street and had come back to visit my old home place, I thanked him for his time, said good-bye, got in my car, and drove away.

A few hours later, I was back in a large, crowded city; then I wound my way along the busy freeways, turned in my rental car at the airport, walked through the boarding chute that put me on an airplane destined for home, and flew away—once again leaving the treasure behind me.

But I had learned something from seeking that treasure, and then almost, but not quite, attaining it. We all have treasures in our lives. Some of us accept them and use them—but most of us leave the best of our selves buried somewhere, waiting to be discovered. *Who knows what could be in that chest?*

For many of us, what we leave behind is the best of us—the best of what we could have been.

I still wish I had broken the lock on that chest way back then, and opened it up. Someday I still may. But what I did then, when I was young, is what many of us do throughout our entire lives. We get a hint of the treasures that are inside ourselves. But at the moment when we could break the lock and let them out, something makes us cover them back up, leaving behind what could have been. Some of us move so far away from where we were, and become so busy with today, that we forget there was ever a treasure in our lives in the first place.

What I learned:

For most of my adult life, I've been telling people about the treasure they have within themselves, and to not walk away or leave it behind, but to seize the moment and bring their treasures

25

to life. Perhaps that's why it was meant to be that the old chest was left in the ground—so it would always be a reminder to me of the treasures that lie buried within each of us, waiting for us to find them. I've become aware, almost daily, that I'm still searching for mine, and that my search will go on as long as I am here.

Chapter Four
The Dock

I was just six years old when something happened that made me think we might have angels watching over us.

I was attending a family reunion, and I was sitting on a dock that reached far out over the water on a wind-chopped lake. It was a dock that stood high above the waves, and the water beneath the dock was deep. I was sitting on the dock not far from my father, who was talking to five or six other men, uncles of mine, who were all sitting on the dock with their backs to the water, enjoying the day, and just talking.

I was wearing my best Sunday pants and sweater. I was also sitting on the edge of the dock with my back to the water, just like the grownups, trying to be like them. While I was listening to the older men talking, I accidentally leaned too far back, and with nothing to grab on to, I frantically clutched nothing but air, and fell backwards, off the edge of the dock, and into the water. This was especially bad; the water was deep, and I didn't know how to swim—and I was wearing heavy clothing that weighted me down.

Whenever I recall this moment, the scene is so vivid in my mind that the entire scene comes rushing back to me, as though I were living it now. My eyes were open as I saw the water rush over me, and as I sank deeper and deeper I saw the streams of sunlight, darkened by the cloudy green color of the water. The huge posts that held the dock were thick with algae, and while I was trying not to breathe or gulp in water, trying desperately not to panic, I tried to use one of the posts that held up the dock to pull myself up toward the light through the water above me. But my hands kept slipping on the heavy green algae slime on the post, and instead of pulling myself higher, I continued to slip down, deeper into the dark water beneath me, and I began to think, in the midst of my panic, that I could not get back up, and I might be drowning.

I remember calling for help in my mind. More than anything in the world, I did not want to die. I fought and fought, but the harder I fought, the deeper I sank. I even remember knowing then, at six years old, that this could be it. This could be where my short life would end, struggling in the deep green water, with no one to save me.

Today, as I think back on it, I cannot even imagine the panic that my six-year-old brain was going through. I know that the deeper I sank, the less hope I had. I remember going down struggling, trying not to gulp in water, thrashing as I went down, and knowing now that I might drown.

I have never been certain what happened next. I was going down, and starting to realize that I could not get out. But something happened, and I'm not sure what it was. Somehow I was saved. To this day, looking back on that moment in my most rational mind, I have no idea how I got back up, out of the deep water, and back up onto the dock which I could not reach.

No one had jumped in to pull me out; no one had even seen me fall in. The dock was far too high, and the slippery post was too slick with algae for me to pull myself up to get out of the water. But somehow, as I lost the last of my air and my lungs could only fill next with lake water, dazed, frightened and confused, I found I was no longer in the water; I was out of the water, and once again sitting back up on the dock.

Later, when I thought about it, I always thought that the angel that pulled me out must have been a strong one—because I found myself once again sitting upright, not far from the place on the dock that I had fallen from, only a few feet away from my father, who was still talking to the other men sitting there. They didn't even know I had been gone. I sat there, water running off of me, shivering and shaking badly, trying to be brave and not cry, coughing up water, too frightened to speak.

My father, who had not seen what had happened, or that I had just almost drowned, turned, and finally noticing me, looked at my drenched Sunday clothes and said, "I thought your mother told you not to get wet."

There was nothing I could say. I just sat shivering, trying to breathe, and couldn't say a word.

And then I looked slowly, back over my shoulder, to see if there was someone there—someone who might have saved me, or helped me get out. But there was nothing there but the water and the waves; at least, no one I could see.

If it was an angel who saved me, and if angels read books, and if that particular angel is reading this one, in case I never said it, I'd like to say it now:

Thank you.

What I learned:

This was my first lesson in recognizing that there is more to life than meets the eye—that there are things we cannot explain; but they are real, and they do happen.

I also learned, fortunately, from this experience when I was very young, that life itself is precious, and it holds a meaning and a purpose for each of us—or we would not be here in the first place. I came to believe that if I had not lived, I would not have fulfilled that purpose. Deep in the dark green water, with sunlight filtering down through it, was where my search for meaning, and my own purpose, began.

Chapter Five
The Tornado

There have been other times I've had help—quite a few of them. But one of those events stands out because it is one that I so easily could have failed to make it through. It is one of the unforgettable moments in my early life.

The small town I was born in was virtually surrounded by endless fields of wheat and other farm crops typical of the Upper Midwest in the United States. My father had a business spraying farmers' fields for weeds and insects that could destroy their crops. The fields were sprayed by specially-rigged tractors with 50-foot-wide sprayer booms, driving carefully up and down the fields, swath after swath, from one end of the field to the other, spraying the field as they drove.

In order for the person driving the tractor to guide the sprayer in a straight line—it had to be exact—the driver sighted on a flag that someone was holding at the far end of the field, and drove straight toward it.

That flag was the reason I spent much of my youth completely alone, in solitude and isolation. I was the kid who waited at the far end of the field, holding the flag.

Being the kid who held the flag meant that while the sprayer tractor made its long, slow crawl from one end of the field to the other and back again, swath after swath, my life was made up of waiting as the minutes and hours crawled by, until the tractor finally appeared again as a distant speck on the horizon, eventually making its way closer and closer to where I was holding the flag. And then, at last, the tractor was there, but only long enough for it to turn around, aiming at another flag on the far opposite end of the field, and then it would slowly disappear again, into the distance.

I worked in those fields from the time I was five years old, barely able to make my way through the grain, until I was well into my teens. Days and months and years of my life were made up of the long, slow minutes waiting each day, as those minutes turned into endless long, slow hours, with one day rolling into the next, with more never-ending fields, more solitude, and nothing to keep me company but the wheat and the sky and my thoughts.

What this meant was that, while my friends from my town were getting together, playing ball (in later years playing pool in the local pool hall), or just hanging out, I was never with them, talking about the things that made their lives evolve; I was out in the farmlands, at the end of some endless wheat field somewhere, talking to myself, and sometimes talking to God.

I don't mention the eternal solitude as a complaint about the way I grew up. It was one of the greatest blessings of my life. To me, life was wheat and fields and birds and sounds (like the breeze rustling through the tassels of the grain), and earth (rich, black loam, teeming with life), and color (entire fields changing tone as clouds passed over them), and sky (big and blue, protecting everything from horizon to horizon in its comforting embrace).

I got really good at watching the weather. I could predict it, perfectly. I knew every kind of cloud, every change in temperature, every subtle shift in the air, from its often empty stillness to any subtle breeze with a shift in direction that would signal the weather was changing.

It was when the sky would darken with the first threatening clouds forming in the northwest, and then moving across the sky, turning it from benevolent to dangerous and then frightening, that I first remember thinking about the role that God and nature played in my safe and secure world out in the fields.

31

One time, when I was at the far end of a very long field, a quarter of a mile from any place of safety, I watched the sky turn from friendly and protecting to dark and threatening, with deep swirls of black and gray clouds dipping lower, closer to the field I was in. I was nine years old at the time, and I remember weighing my chances of making it to safety as the sky turned black, and the wind picked up strangely, moving first in one direction, and then another.

I also remember, at the time, talking to God about it. I was first excited about the display of dark clouds, stark and black, moving swiftly across a diminishing bright, safe, blue sky. But then the entire sky above me started going black, and then the lightning began to light up the threatening clouds, flashing brightly, rapid and staccato, from cloud to cloud and to the ground. There was no rain yet, but I could see it coming toward me, sweeping across the fields in the distance, a giant curtain of gray, blanketing everything in its path.

The reason I talked to God about this one is because, having lived out in the fields for several years by then, and having experienced every kind of weather possible, I had never seen anything quite like this before. In all my youthful moments of figuring out nature, I had never once seen a sky that looked this menacing.

I could not see the sprayer tractor in the distance. The driver, I knew, would have turned around to get back to the base point at the other end of the field where the water-tanker truck waited near a grove of trees and farm buildings, and the equipment would have to be protected and taken care of. I knew, in my nine-year-old mind, that there would be no truck or tractor making its way across the field, trying to find me and bring me in. The change in the sky had happened too fast, and they would know that I would probably go to ground, lay flat, and hope that whatever was coming would pass over me.

I remember the mental movie of this moment because, to this day, it remains indelibly wired into my brain. I talked out loud with God. What should I do? And in my talk with God, as the black shifting clouds seemed to moan and roar increasingly louder and louder, my mind kept returning to one thought: *tornado!*

In that moment, the direction was loud and clear. Something, or someone, told me to run. *Don't drop down; don't try to lie flat. Run! Run as fast as you can, and don't stop.*

So that's what I did. I ran.

It is entirely possible that, as my reader, you may never have experienced what it's like to be a rather small nine-year-old kid, and having to run through a wheat field. The wheat, at that time of year, was above my waist. So running wasn't really running. It was running in a leaping kind of way, trying to keep my legs from being constantly entangled in the weaves of the wheat, not fall, move as fast as I could, and *keep* moving.

I had grown up in a part of the world where everyone learns about tornados. My own aunt and uncle's home had been lifted off its foundation and torn away while the two of them and their three children had huddled in the northwest corner of their basement. The tornado had pulled the glasses off my aunt's face, but left her and all of her family safe. That was a miracle . . . and a miracle was what I needed now.

Within minutes, the entire sky had gone black—a deep, dark, green black that I had never seen before. As I continued to run, struggling through the wheat, the sound from the sky, now all around me, changed from moaning and thundering to a deep, frightening roar, like a dozen freight trains, and I realized that what was happening in nature was bigger than I was, and I might not make it to anywhere safe.

It seemed to take forever to fight the wheat and keep running when the wheat tried to wrap itself around my ankles and my feet. The roar from above me and around me was so loud that I knew this was something very real, and I had to keep my mind working if I was going to survive.

It was almost exactly the same time that the rain hit—a torrent of it—that I saw the tractor and the big water-tank truck not more than a hundred yards in front of me across the wheat. The wind and rain were now coming from every direction, and hard. I was already soaked in the driving, drenching rain, but all I had to do was get there.

Both the tractor driver and the water truck driver were trying to wrap up hoses and secure all of the equipment when I got close enough for them to see me in the downpour and the roar of the wind, which, by now, had gotten even worse.

After I had heard the voice telling me to run, and heeding its advice, I had made my way through the torrent of wind and rain across the field.

I attribute what I did next to help from my angels. A tractor has large rear wheels, heavy steel wheels with rubber tires around them, and they are sometimes concave in design—in which the iron wheel has a large indentation next to the axle that creates a concave space just big enough for a small nine-year-old boy to fit into. With the wind whipping into an even greater frenzy, the sound of the storm was now a scream. At the last possible moment, I jumped into the concave space of the tractor's rear left wheel, wrapped my arms around its heavy steel spokes, held on for dear life, closed my eyes, and prayed.

As soon as they saw that I was in the wheel-well of the tractor, one of the drivers jumped into the cab of the water-tank truck. The tractor/sprayer driver had wanted to get me to a safer place, but by now the banshee scream of the wind was at decibels so loud that no one's voice could be heard, no matter how loudly they were shouting at you.

As the first dark, angry swirl of the tornado twisted its way into our small encampment, I opened my eyes, and the picture that remains in my mind of that moment is George, the tractor driver, holding on to the back of the water truck, as his entire body was lifted sideways, spread out completely horizontal, the wind screaming, trying to pull him away, and George never letting go.

It was no more than twenty minutes later, after I had clung to the inside of the tractor wheel, and George had almost been carried away by the tornado, that we walked again on the stable earth, and looked at the damage all around us.

In the nearby grove, a pathway of trees was uprooted and twisted, as only a tornado will do. Grain bins, usually round with a peaked metallic roof, were thrown and torn as though a giant hand had smashed them in a rage. A windmill tower, not a hundred feet from us, was twisted on itself like a corkscrew. A farmer's barn that had stood solid and strong through decades of previous storms was shattered and splintered into kindling.

And across the wheat field we saw the twisting, turning track where the tornado had gone, pulling wheat from the ground as it went. The track wound its way across the field *directly to where I had been standing when the voice told me to run, just a few brief minutes earlier.*

The most vivid images I took away from the experience are those of standing at the far end of that field alone, as the clouds changed and the tornado's forces took hold, being told to run— not to lie down, but to run—the life-changing event of running through the wheat field to find sanctuary in the concave steel of a tractor wheel, and seeing the after-track of where the tornado had gone when it wound its way through the wheat. I had again been saved from an almost certain demise, by something much bigger than me.

To my angels: *Thank you again.*

What I learned:
This remarkable experience was a reminder to me of both my insignificance and my value. In that storm I was no more than a

thatch of wheat that could have just as easily been carried away by the wind. And yet, I wasn't. And, like being saved from drowning, I believed there was a reason that I was spared. At least, I like to think so. The experience of making it through a devastating tornado was a perfect and timely reminder.

This was also when I started becoming consciously aware of "*listening.*" Had I not *listened* in the field, I would not have heard the voice that told me to run. It was the same voice that I would learn to recognize and listen to many times, in many different ways, in my life.

This was my first awareness of the power of intuition, or tuning into the higher consciousness or spirit that is within each of us, but that we have to learn to hear. I was fortunate that when I heard the voice in the storm, it was not a whisper; it was a shout. And it got my attention in a way I would never forget.

Chapter Six
The Bully

Most of us have had to deal with bullies in our lives at one time or another. The first time I had to deal with a serious bully was in middle school. I mention the incident here, both because bullies should never be tolerated, and also because I was surprised by how my youthful self decided to handle the problem.

Ralph was a bully who stepped right out of central casting. If there were a handbook for bullies, Ralph had studied it—if he could even read. He was big, mean, and had a pack of followers. Meanwhile, I was small for my age, close to frail, had no followers, and to make matters worse, I wore glasses!

What made Ralph frightening was that, after taunting someone for a week or two, he would call them out for no reason, and tell them that he would be waiting for them outside the school gym after the last afternoon class. Then he and his group would wait there, usually on the steps outside the gymnasium, until his prey came out the large double school doors, and he would then taunt the poor subject more, and start pushing him until he got a fight started, which Ralph would always win.

The teachers usually didn't know what was going on, and none of the kids would say anything to a teacher about the bullying, because Ralph would always tell the kid that if he told a teacher, he would get twice the beating.

Ralph fit the profile of being a "serial bully." That is, he would terrify someone until it ended up with him beating the other kid, badly, in a fight. Then, with his distorted need for power satiated for a time, he would back off until his need would rise again, and another victim would slip innocently into his view, and it would start all over again.

I went about my life without worrying about Ralph too much, because he had never gotten me in his cross-hairs. Until he decided it was my time.

He started out, just as he did with each of his victims, by taunting me in the hallways between classes, and that led to him shoving me into other kids, pulling my glasses off my face and holding them just higher than I could reach, and then knocking all of my schoolbooks out of my arms and laughing with his pals while I picked up my books from where they lay scattered across the hallway floor. Ralph's favorite thing was making kids drop their books.

Ralph was a quintessential, low-self-esteem, small-mind-in-a-big-body bully, just like thousands of other bullies that populate every school and playground in the country. His taunting of me went on for days, and each day it got worse—that was Ralph's M.O.—until he was waiting in ambush so he could grab my assignment papers and tear them into shreds when I was on my way into the class where I was supposed to hand in the assignment.

I knew now that it was only a matter of time before Ralph would stage his after school fight on the gymnasium steps, and I was, by then, living each day in fear of when that would happen. I knew I wouldn't be able to defend myself, and I knew there would be no escaping what was going to take place. I was going to be beaten, maybe badly, by a kid who belonged in reform school, while his equally tough-minded friends cheered him on.

Then, one day, I was sitting in my desk just before class started, and I smelled a foul breath odor as someone leaned down from behind me and whispered in my ear. It was Ralph—and it was time.

"Meet me on the gym steps after school," he hissed in my ear. "I'm going to beat your ass."

I sat rigidly still in my seat, my heart pounding. I had less than three hours of classes until I was going to be beaten on the gymnasium steps in front of Ralph's crowd of friends. I felt like Caesar on the Ides of March, if Caesar had known in advance what was going to happen next.

Those three hours dragged on, and in the hallway between classes, the only time I saw Ralph, he just grinned a maniacal grin and loudly punched his one fist into his other hand, expressing the height of his communication skills.

I was maybe half Ralph's size; I was not bulked up; I had never taken up boxing, and I knew that by his "rules," I would lose.

That is, by *his* rules—but not by *mine*. I had one thing going for me. I had grown up being taught to be creative. And that's what I would have to do now. I wouldn't run; I wouldn't hide; but I was not going to lose.

About ten minutes before the end of the last class of the day, I went up to the teacher's desk and asked to be excused because I wasn't feeling well. The teacher glanced up at me, noticed I looked kind of ashen white, assumed I was sick, and said I could go.

I gathered up my books and left the classroom. Then I walked to my locker and opened it, and pulled out every book I owned. I closed my locker and walked down the hallway toward the double gymnasium doors, opened them, and walked outside.

There was no one there yet, waiting for me, but in a few minutes the bell would sound, and out they would come, ready for another one-sided spectacle fight.

On each side of the gymnasium steps was a large brick and stone abutment about four feet high. I took my stack of books and hefted them up to the top of the abutment. Then I climbed up. Above the gymnasium steps was a large concrete and metal overhang, like a theater marquee, and I picked up my armload of books and pushed them onto the top of the marquee. Then I reached up with both hands and pulled myself up, and struggled my way onto the flat rooftop of the marquee.

At three-thirty pm, the end-of-class bell sounded, the last one of the day. In another minute, students began pouring out of the big gymnasium doors. While most of the kids headed for home, a group of a dozen or so students came out of the building laughing and shoving each other around, and then formed a loose semi-circle out from the front of the steps, waiting for their leader, and the fight he had planned.

In another minute or two, Ralph pushed the gym doors open and swaggered out to greet his throng. He stepped down two or three granite steps toward the sidewalk, and then swung around, looking for someone.

He was looking for me. I knew that because he shouted my name out a couple of times, and when he still didn't see me coming through the doors, he added a few adjectives to my name. I think "Bulls..t scaredy-cat," was one of them. Then he said, "I knew he wouldn't show. He's too scared. He's too chickens..t to deal with me."

It was at that moment that I stood up, directly above Ralph on the outer edge of the marquee roof. His gang of friends saw me, and the tall stack of heavy books I was holding out in front of me, and they looked kind of shocked. Ralph saw the look on their faces, but he had no idea what they were looking at.

From up above him, I said just one word, quietly. I said his name, "Ralph."

Ralph's favorite thing was making kids drop their books.
When Ralph looked up, and when we made eye contact, I dropped every book I was holding out in front of me, straight down, on his head.

Ralph hit the steps pretty hard. And when he went down, he didn't get back up. I climbed back down over the edge of the marquee roof, to the top of the brick abutment, and then down to the concrete floor above the steps. I then walked down the steps to Ralph, who was still lying, sprawled out, where he had planned to bloody and humiliate me. He would be fine, but he still looked a little dazed when I knelt down beside him—and whispered in his ear, *"Don't ever bully anyone again."*

Then I gathered up my books, stood up, and looked at the circle of Ralph's friends, who were still kind of in shock. Not one of them took a single step forward. No one spoke. They had just seen their hero, in one moment, taken out by someone half his size.

With my books in hand, I walked down the rest of the steps, onto the sidewalk, took one look back at Ralph, who was just now slowly getting up, and I walked home.

Ralph and his friends never bothered me again.

Ralph's bullying also dropped off noticeably to an occasional word to someone now and then, but he seemed to have lost his enthusiasm for picking on small, smart kids who wore glasses. And I also noticed that after class each day, Ralph usually avoided using the gymnasium steps, and when he did use them, he would cautiously look up above his head to the marquee, just before he carefully walked down the steps.

What I learned:

While I would never recommend that anyone drop a stack of books on someone, I was thankful that, in that case, being creative may have saved me from a broken nose or a much more serious injury.

What I learned most, of course, is how false most bullies really are—and they remain so today, with bullying in epidemic proportions. It is one of those universal failings of society that I would still like to do something about.

Chapter Seven
The Dance

Sometimes there are people who step into your life just because it's time for you to learn something, and they're the person who was chosen to teach you.

I was fourteen when I had my first chance to go to a dance. It was a dance at our school, the Junior Prom, held at a time before middle schools had replaced junior high schools.

I grew up in a non-dancing family. Our religion didn't forbid dancing exactly, but my father was brought up in a strict Lutheran home—my grandfather was a Lutheran minister—and my father thought that dancing was not a Heavenly pursuit, so in our family it was not allowed. But I decided to attend the Junior Prom, and carefully avoided bringing up the matter to my father.

A greater problem was, who would I ask to go to the dance, and—more important—who would I ask that would say *yes*? At the time, sitting every day in the large study hall in our school, there was one female I noticed a lot. And she was the one person in the entire school that I thought I would most like to take to the Junior Prom. She was the cutest girl in school. She was Miss Kelly, the study hall teacher.

Miss Kelly was sharp, intelligent, athletic, and cute. She was also the girls' physical education teacher, and everything I could imagine in a girl. I had no comprehension that a student could not take his study hall teacher to the Junior High School Prom. I don't think it occurred to me that there was something called "convention," unwritten rules or borderlines that you didn't cross. If there were lines, I didn't see them.

The next day in study hall, after I had decided I was going to invite Miss Kelly as my date to the prom, I sat in my study hall desk, trying to figure out a way to ask her. I could go up and talk to her at the big counter she sat behind. But if I did that, and it didn't go well, everyone in study hall would be watching, and I didn't want to go down in defeat in front of all my classmates.

But then I had an idea. I wrote a note on a piece of notebook paper. It said, "Dear Miss Kelly. Would you like to go to the Junior Prom with me?" And then I printed my name and under that I signed it. I folded the note twice and thought about what to do next.

I looked around me, and finally I turned to Paul, a classmate of mine, and said, "Paul, would you take this message up to Miss Kelly?"

I saw that Paul didn't really understand the importance of the role he was playing in the universal order of things, because he just said "Sure," took my note, and walked to the front of the study hall, and when Miss Kelly looked up, handed my note to her.

While Paul ambled back to his desk, not knowing that he had possibly just played a part in shifting the forces of destiny, I sat petrified in my seat, watching Miss Kelly's every move and facial expression as she read my note.

She read the note once, and then I could see that she read it again. Then she picked up her pen, thought for a bit, and wrote something on the note. When she had finished writing, she folded the note back up, and said, "Paul, please come to the front."

Paul got up, walked back up to the front counter, and accepted the folded note that Miss Kelly placed in his hand. Then Paul, just as uninterested as before, ambled back to his seat, slouched down in his usual position, held out his hand with the note in it, and said, "Here. I guess this is for you."

I took the note and turned away for some privacy before I opened it. When I did, I read the words that enlivened my day.

43

The words Miss Kelly had written on my note were: "*Speak for yourself, John,*" a quote from Longfellow's *The Courtship of Miles Standish*, which we had studied in English class. And then, under that, she had written one word: "*Yes.*"

I should mention that in the days of Miss Kelly and students like me who were infatuated with their teachers, it was not the world of troubled teachers and students we sometimes have in our very different world today. Now, everyone and every connection between people can be suspect. But at the time, there was none of that. It was a simpler world, and a lot more innocent. I had wanted to take someone to the Junior Prom—I had asked her, and she had said yes. It was as simple as that.

I still don't know if my father ever learned that his fourteen-year-old son was actually going to a dance, and that he was taking his study hall teacher as his date. If my father ever knew, he never said a word. And if he knew and never said a word, it was because my mother, who had once loved to dance, had put her foot down on the matter.

On the day of the Junior Prom, Miss Kelly was going to pick me up in her car at seven p.m. At about three o'clock in the afternoon I had started to become concerned about the flower corsage I wanted to give her. I knew that you should give your prom date flowers, and I had none to give her. I couldn't afford anything like roses, or a florist's corsage, so an hour before my date was supposed to arrive, one of my older sisters helped me make a small arrangement of lilacs, the flowers that grew in abundance on the bushes outside our home, and I was ready.

I was also in my Prom best. I didn't have a tuxedo, but I had my Sunday church pants, white shirt, no tie, and jacket, and I probably looked okay.

When Miss Kelly arrived to pick me up in her late model Chevy, she waited for me to exit my home, and walk cool and confidently out to her car. I got in and gave her the lilac corsage, and she took a minute to put it on. She checked it out in the rear view mirror, and then she put the car in reverse and pulled out of the driveway. As we drove away, I think I saw someone watching from every window of my house.

When we arrived at the dance, Miss Kelly was a perfect picture of class. She introduced me as her date to everyone, even though they all knew me well. She asked me if I would get some punch for the two of us, and I did, and we sat on two of the folding chairs around the dance floor and had the punch and the cookies that I had gotten.

Oddly, no one questioned or raised an eyebrow that we were at the prom together. Even the other teachers smiled and chatted with us, and I felt like a real adult, someone really old and experienced, like maybe someone twenty years old.

I did notice that my reputation with my classmates had suddenly gone up. Instead of making fun, they were being polite, almost respectful.

As the evening progressed, everything was going fine, but I was beginning to get nervous because they were starting to play dance music, and I was aware that I had never mentioned to Miss Kelly that I had never danced a single step in my life.

Because of this, I put off the inevitable by not asking her to dance. But eventually, that ploy didn't work because after half an hour of my not dancing with her, Miss Kelly turned to me and asked, "Would you like to dance?"

"Sure," I said, and stood up.

We walked to the dance floor. She turned and faced me, and I faced her, and I stood there, not having a single idea what to do. This was in the days before you could just move around and wave your arms to dance. This was when you addressed your partner, one arm raised and holding her hand in the air, the other arm lightly on her waist, and actually took steps and moved in common.

45

It took Miss Kelly only moments to recognize that I had absolutely no idea what to do. Good person that she was, she took my hand, said very quietly but warmly, "Follow me," and walked the two of us inconspicuously off the dance floor, out through the double swinging doors of the gymnasium, down the dimly-lighted marble hallway, down a short flight of steps, and into an almost dark empty hallway in the grade school part of the building.

We could still hear the dance music coming from the gymnasium, and it was the only sound in the dark, empty corridor, until Miss Kelly said, "Put your right hand on my shoulder. Put your left hand here. Look at your feet and make sure they're just a little way apart, and then don't ever look at them again. Now look up, look at me, and you're going to take one step forward, one step sliding to the right, one step back, and one step sliding back to the left. Got it? Okay, here we go."

For the next half hour, while the Junior Prom music echoed hauntingly down the long, empty marble hallway somewhere in the darkened grade school part of the school building, that lady taught me how to stand, how to step, how to turn, and how to dance.

By the end of the Prom evening, Miss Kelly's lilac corsage had wilted badly, but she did not take it off, and she did not mention it, other than to say how wonderful lilacs smelled. When she drove me home, she waited in the driveway to make sure I got in safely. Then she slowly backed her car out of the driveway, and pulled away. I stood inside the door and watched her tail lights dim into the distance.

Then I went into the house, which was dark, and quietly made my way to my bedroom.

Just before I went in, from the bedroom next door, I heard my sister Holly's voice. "How did it go?" she whispered.

I whispered back, "I learned how to dance."

What I learned:

I learned more than how to dance; I learned about dignity. An important part of the quality of life is about dignity. How to offer dignity to others is an art that more people should know. Miss Kelly was a good teacher; she not only had dignity, she knew how to share it with others. Instead of making me feel foolish, or embarrassed, she created a perfect object lesson in dignity, and how to treat others with respect, no matter who they are. Even a fourteen-year-old boy—whom she taught not only how to dance, but also, with dignity, how to begin to become a man.

Chapter Eight
The Time Machine

I was fifteen when I first learned to *not* talk to other boys my age about anything to do with what would later be popularized as quantum physics. At the time, advanced physics wasn't a popular subject among school kids, and I wouldn't really begin to understand it until much later. But my first short step into that world taught me a lesson I would not forget.

After school one day, a few of my friends came over to my home to hang out on the lawn and do nothing. I took advantage of this opportunity to talk to my friends about something that had been on my mind a lot lately: the idea that time didn't actually exist, and that all of us existed in a world where time was only a concept—not real—and that everything that had ever happened in the past or would happen in the future was happening right now. But we didn't know that, because all we could see was our own "right now," even though all the other "right nows" from the past, the present, and the future were all happening at the same time.

My school friends thought the whole idea was crazy, and after some typical pushing and shoving and tough-talking smart guy group dominance techniques by one or two of the other members of the group, I had been put in my place, and would know, forever, that my idea was nothing more than stupid, and we should do something more important, like throwing knives into the bark on one of the pine trees that surrounded my home.

But then, still thinking physics, I had a brilliant idea! "I can show you how time works!" I said to my friends.

The success of my idea would be based on breaking one of my father's rules that had to do with his photographic slide collection——which was *sacred*.

My father's love of photography had come to life when he bought a 35mm camera. At one time, long before digital cameras were built into phones, people took photographs on cameras that held a roll of 35mm film. When the film was processed, you received a box of 35mm "slides," positive color exposures, each photograph mounted in a two-inch-square cardboard frame.

To view your photographs you had to run them through a slide projector that projected the picture onto a screen. And to make that easy, the color photo slides could be placed in a slide tray, the most popular of which was a circular tray that held 100 slides. Lock the tray full of slides into the projector, turn it on, and *voila*, a slide show.

Fathers at the time had a common bond, spending hours putting everyone to sleep while they proudly narrated slides of family reunions or last summer's vacation. My own father was in that group of slide show givers, but he had taken his hobby to a higher level.

He would spend hours arranging and rearranging hundreds of slides into circular Kodak Carousel plastic slide trays. When he had a perfect sequence of a hundred slides, all in order, he would put the circular locking cap on the round carousel tray, and carefully place the tray in its own box in a special file cabinet drawer reserved exclusively for his collection.

And then, as he often would, he would restate his absolute rule that no one, *ever*, for any reason, could open that special file cabinet drawer, let alone ever *touch* one of his boxed stacks of slide carousels. Those perfectly organized 35mm slide photographs were his treasure, and he protected them beyond anything else of value that he owned. No one could touch them. Ever.

It was that rule that I would have to break if I wanted to explain my "theory of time" to my classmates, and although I may have realized what I was doing at the time, I must have believed that it was worth the risk I was taking. I went into my home, waited until my mother wasn't watching, bravely walked straight to the filing cabinet, opened the sacred top drawer, reached in and extracted a sacred box containing a sacred slide carousel filled with a hundred sacred 35mm slides.

With the proof of my argument that "time doesn't actually exist" in my hands, I walked back outside, where my friends were still throwing knives into the tree, and yelled, "*I can prove it!*"

"*Prove what?*" they asked.

"*This!*" I answered, and opened the box and held out the circular tray that held a hundred of my father's slides. I walked up to them and carefully unscrewed the locking ring that held all the slides securely in place, and held up the tray of slides for all of them to see.

Once I had their attention, I selected the first slide in the tray and lifted it out. "Imagine that this is a photograph of Adam and Eve in the Garden of Eden," I said, holding the first slide up to them for a moment, and then putting it carefully back in its appropriate slot in the tray. I moved my hand a short way around the circular tray, selected another slide and pulled it out. "This is Christopher Columbus discovering America." I held the slide up for a moment, to let the idea sink in, and then replaced it into its slot in the tray. I then moved a little farther around the tray and pulled out a third slide. "This is Lincoln giving the Gettysburg Address," I said, holding the slide up so that you could imagine that if you looked at it closely you would be able to see Lincoln on a stage in Gettysburg, Pennsylvania, on November 19, 1863.

I put Lincoln back into his slot in the carousel and moved on, selecting another slide to hold up to them. "This is Pearl Harbor on December 7, 1941," once again letting them imagine with me what was captured on that slide. I moved on and extracted another slide. "This is right now. It's a picture of us, after school today on today's date." And then I pulled out one final slide and held it up to them. "And this is us twenty-five years from now. In the future, when we're all old men."

"Think about it," I said to them. "All of those things that are happening in those slides are real. And all of them are happening right now. It's like this is a time machine. It just depends on which slide you take out and look at."

Dead silence. I don't remember thinking the word "stunned," but stunned is what I saw on the faces of my friends. I may have even thought, "*Yes! They got it!*"

But a couple of moments later I realized maybe they *didn't* get it when one of them pushed me, and yelled something like "stupid s..t" and then someone else joined in, pushing me in the other direction, shouting that I was crazy. I was trying to protect myself but, more important, I was trying to protect my father's sacred carousel of slides. And then another of my friends pushed me from behind, and with my hands going out in front of me, I saw the slide tray and all its slides fly out of my hands.

In that moment, in front of my eyes, in time-stopping slow motion, I saw the slides fly out of the carousel, and begin to fall toward the ground. In those slow-motion moments, instead of seeing just regular slides, I saw Adam and Eve, and the building of the pyramids, and the black plague in Europe, and King John signing the Magna Carta, and Joan of Arc riding into battle, and Cortez conquering the Aztecs, and Thomas Jefferson writing the Declaration of Independence, and an astronaut walking on the moon sometime in the future, and one day my own children graduating from school . . .

And then time shuddered to a stop, and all of the slides landed, scattered on the ground.

It was the first time I had ever felt completely alone in a world filled with people. I stood there, looking down at the ruin of slides, all one hundred of them, scattered around the empty time machine on the ground in front of me, my shirt pocket torn in the scuffle, and a bloodied lip that I didn't even feel.

Without saying another word, I began to pick up the sacred slides, one by one, and fit them back into the slots in the slide carousel. There wasn't a chance that I could get the slides put back into the perfect sequence my father had arranged them in. I just put them in, one by one, and when I had all of them brushed off and in the carousel, I walked into my home, opened the file cabinet drawer, and put the sacred slides back in their place, and closed the drawer.

A little later my mother came in and daubed my broken lip with a damp cloth, and that evening, she mended my torn shirt. I had expected the consequences to be very bad. Breaking my father's rule about never touching his photographic slides was an inexcusable offense. So it was strange to me, for a long time afterward, that my father never said a single word about the slides. It was never mentioned.

I think my mother may have been watching from the window.

What I learned:
At the time of this experience, I first thought I had learned only to keep my mouth shut, and keep my ideas and discoveries about universal truths to myself. But the more I thought about the experience, the more I thought I needed to learn how to present my ideas in ways that other people would be able to understand and accept—not just discoveries about the relativity of time—but any idea that might be new or foreign to someone else.

This experience would begin to train me to listen to other people's thoughts and beliefs *first*, so that when I presented my own thoughts or positions, those ideas could find a common bond with the people I was talking to. And *that* lesson—to learn to understand others and how *they* think—has done more to help me get ideas across in books and in public speaking than any other lesson I have learned.

Chapter Nine
Speaking to the Wheat

It was when I was working in the wheat fields when I was young, that I learned public speaking. Almost everything I needed to learn about speaking—something that years later, I would spend much of my life doing—I learned by speaking to the wheat.

I wanted to learn to speak to crowds of any size, without fear or hesitation. If I was going follow my dream to help change the world, I would have to learn to speak with strength, and poise, and confidence.

In the small town I lived in, there was little chance for me to learn and practice the skill of speaking. But destiny remedied that problem by placing me in front of endless imaginary audiences of eager listeners—the fields of wheat I worked in as a boy.

Arranging to put me in wheat fields was not a random choice for destiny to make; doing that would prove to be profoundly important to the growth of my dream and to how I would bring that dream to life. But it all began in the wheat fields.

Interestingly, wheat has a peculiar characteristic of sounding very much like a live audience. When a soft wind blows through a wheat field, the tassels of seed pods at the top of the wheat plants rub against each other in the breeze, making a soft rushing sound, like a large audience applauding. The stronger the breeze, the louder the applause. So I had, at the time, a tremendous determination to learn, and an audience ready to applaud anytime a breeze wafted through the field.

And it was in the wheat that I learned public speaking. Each day, you would find me in some wheat field, a young boy with so many dreams to fulfill, practicing every motion, every movement, every step, every gesture that I believed would help me speak.

I taught myself the difference between "palms out" gestures, which I knew would push the audience away, and a "palms in," welcoming gesture, which I sensed would pull the listeners toward me.

I discovered that every detailed motion of my hands would, in itself, communicate a message beyond the words that were being spoken. I learned to express my thoughts in each motion, each step I took, the tilt and turn of my head, the extra force of a chest full of breath, and the calm reassurance of a lowered brow, with eyes still strong and penetrating, looking directly into the eyes of the listeners.

It was in the wheat fields that I learned the difference between a broad, strong motion of my arms, elbows out, palms down and hands forward, and the softer, beckoning call for affirmation, elbows in and palms widespread and out, like a preacher welcoming parishioners to an altar call.

Sometimes, when I was speaking, working at being eloquent, a breeze would rise up in the field, and I would hear *the sound*. At first it was just a whisper, and then it would grow, like an audience that begins to applaud, and then it would build, with the wind growing, the tassels of the wheat moving against one another with more strength and motion, until it became a cheering throng, the wheat nodding and bowing in the breeze, applauding wildly in great approval.

I knew at the time, of course, that it wasn't the words I was saying that were creating the "applause." That would have to come later. At first, when I was speaking to the wheat, I was saying anything that came to my mind, streams of consciousness starting nowhere and ending anywhere, just words, meaning nothing, spoken to no one real, waiting for applause that came in on the next breeze that drifted over the field. But it was also out in those wheat fields that I began to think about things like logic, and syntax, and idea development. And in time it was true—almost everything I learned about public speaking, I learned from speaking to the wheat.

It was many years later, long after I had left the wheat fields, and left those memories far behind me, and had grown up and moved on into my later career, that I was, on one occasion, speaking to an audience of several thousand people in the city of Katowice, in the country of Poland.

I was particularly aware of this experience for two reasons. The first was that I recognized during my talk that I was standing on the exact same stage, on the exact same spot, that not too many years previously, a Communist Party official had been standing, talking to the same people about what they could *not* do—about the *limitations* in their lives.

And I was there now, standing on the same stage, talking to the same people about what they *could* do, and how *unlimited* their lives could be.

Years earlier, I had set a goal to speak in the Soviet Union, or behind the Iron Curtain, in countries like Poland, because of the personal freedom that my message was about. And when the Soviet Union was no more, I wanted to bring my message to that part of the world more than ever. And now, here I was in Poland, and it had finally happened.

The other thing I was clearly aware of, speaking to this audience, was that because I was speaking English to a Polish audience, everything I said had to be translated, and then repeated to the audience in Polish, after each few sentences I spoke. To accomplish this, there were three translators sitting in the center of the front row of the audience. At times, after I had said something, the translators would talk between themselves, making sure they got every meaning and nuance of what I was expressing exactly right. So it was, that during this particular presentation of my message, I had the unusual opportunity to pause, to think and reflect, while what I had just said was being translated and spoken to the audience.

It was during one of those long pauses, after I had said a few sentences, and the translators had just begun to deliver my message to the crowd, that I heard the sound.

At first it was just a whisper—as the audience began to applaud—and then the applause built, and then it grew, like a soft breeze in a wheat field, the tassels of the wheat moving against one another with more strength and motion, until it became a cheering throng, the wheat nodding and bowing in the breeze, applauding in great approval.

And in that moment, I was no longer on a stage speaking to a huge audience in Katowice, Poland. I was back in the wheat fields of my youth, a young boy, speaking to the wheat, with so many dreams to fulfill, stepping and moving and gesturing, finding an honest, natural way, so that one day I could talk to any audience, anywhere, and speak not only from the heart and caring of a man who was talking to the world, but from the soul of a boy who was talking only to the wheat.

What I learned:

There are two things I learned that are woven together in the experience of talking to the wheat as a young boy, and then, in this instance, talking to an audience in Poland.

The first lesson is about visualization; by practicing speaking in the fields, without realizing it at the time, I was practicing visualizing my dreams—and in fact, in speaking to the wheat I was literally *living* my future, in my mind, in advance. As I grew older, because I had grown so accustomed to practicing seeing myself in the future, I began to visualize accomplishing any goal I set, and living that achievement in my mind, long before the goal was reached. (As a boy, I had no idea that visualization would become one of the most popular "success" techniques that would later be taught.)

A parallel lesson I learned was that each of us creates most of the realities that happen in our lives. It was no accident that I was on that stage in Poland; I had begun to create that reality when I first began talking to wheat fields—having absolutely no idea that one day I would have the chance to actually bring to life what I was practicing in my mind. The lesson is not a new one to the field of personal growth, but it is a profound lesson nevertheless—that we are creating our tomorrow, by what we are thinking today.

Chapter Ten
My Grandfather's Shoes

I am standing on another stage, this one in Sacramento, California. There are nineteen thousand people seated in the vast audience in front of me. The huge event center is filled, and I am alone on the stage, dwarfed by three giant projection screens, one behind me and one on each side of the large stage. The screens project close-up pictures of me twenty feet tall. I'm not nervous, but I pause before I begin to speak, and look down in thought. I make sure I have "that feeling" that always tells me I am in the right place in my mind, ready to speak for the right reasons.

I had known I was going to speak to audiences since I was very young. The vision itself may have gotten started when I was just a toddler, sitting with my parents and siblings in the front row of my grandfather's church, listening to him speak to his congregation. I was so young that all I remembered of my grandfather at first were his shoes. The toes of those shoes were always shiny and black as he stood in front of the congregation. Being a small child, I was propped into the church pew, and from that vantage point what I saw most of my grandfather was from his knees to the floor, so I suppose I studied what I saw most—his shoes.

As I grew older I got over being frightened to death of my grandfather's thundering voice. (During church services he projected so loudly that I thought he was angry, and yelling at everyone.) In time I began to understand what he was saying, and as I continued to grow older I developed an early and lasting respect for him. He was a true patriarch, strong-minded, with an ethic for hard work, and that ethic ran through his family.

Oddly, one of the most difficult challenges of my youth, from early childhood through high school, was that I, myself, almost never had good shoes to wear. Never any shoes like my grandfather's. Growing up in what we would now call a poverty home, one of the most embarrassing things in my life was having to wear my older *sister's* hand-me-down shoes to school when I had no shoes to wear of my own. (Kids can be cruel. You can imagine the taunting I got from the other students when I was wearing my sister's shoes. Hearing their whispers in school each day was always humiliating.) But even when I wore boys' shoes, they would wear out long before my parents could afford to buy new ones.

Working in the fields, my shoes almost always had holes in them, where the shoe leather on the sides of the shoes would break loose from the sole, and stones and pebbles would work their way in, and I was constantly either limping along with stones in my shoes, or shaking one foot or the other, trying to get the dirt and pebbles out.

Many years later, as an adult, when I was speaking professionally on stage, I bought a pair of shoes that were identical to those my grandfather had worn. I polished the long slender toe section of those shoes to a spotless shine in the hotel room each morning that I was scheduled to speak. It was not just that they were great looking professional footwear; they were a true metaphor for doing my best to fill those shoes.

Today, each time I'm preparing to speak, before I walk down the long hallways from my hotel room to the ballroom where I will be speaking, I follow a consistent routine in preparation.

The most important part of getting ready to speak before an event, after I get dressed and ready for the stage, is when I go into a mental zone of preparation. I think specifically about the people who will be attending that day. I focus on them until I have a clear picture of them in my mind, sitting in the audience, waiting for me to present my message. Then I change my focus to see them at home, or working, doing their best to make their lives happy and secure. I also see them when they have problems and are trying to get through them. I see them wanting to make things better, and eager to improve if they can.

By doing this, I find that I never talk to an "*audience*;" I talk to *people*, *real* people, individuals with lives and families and problems and hopes and dreams, and they are never a group of nameless people; they are individuals, and I talk to them one-to-one.

At each speaking event, just before I leave my room to walk down the hallway, I think one final thought: "If these people were all my closest personal friends and family, and if I had only this one last time to speak to them, what would I tell them?" And with those words in my mind, I enter the speaking room, or backstage at the bigger events, say a silent prayer that I will say exactly the right words, meditate in silence, wait for the voice over the loudspeakers of the person introducing me, walk up the steps onto the stage area, walk to the center of the stage and look out—and there they are.

I've just been introduced to the audience, and I've walked to the center of the stage. I'm standing in front of the nineteen thousand people in the huge arena, all waiting to see if I'm real, or if I'm not, or if they should really listen, or if they should tune out. As I say thank you to the person who introduced me, I'm looking out over the vast throng, and I see them, all the real people, with real lives, and real problems, and real hopes and real dreams, each of them waiting to learn if I have ideas that could help them get better.

Now, as I look out to them, I notice how incredibly quiet it has become in this great arena. It's almost perfectly silent now.

And I think about how real and important each individual in the audience is.

I then step back for a moment, and I look down.

But I'm not looking down out of shyness or humility. *I'm looking at my shoes.* And I see that they look exactly like my grandfather's elegant black shoes, the toes spotless and shined to perfection. In spirit, he is here with me now.

And then I look up again, my eyes moving across the faces. And just before I'm about to speak, I pause, a long, extended pause that lets them see inside of me. And then I say what I came here to say.

What I learned:

The most important lesson I've learned about audiences is that they aren't a *group* of people; to me an audience is made up of its separate individuals, each of whom is there with his or her own heart and soul and mind. Reaching each of those individuals starts and ends with caring for each of them, whether I know them personally or not. The way I look at life, we are all one. When I see each of those individuals in the audience, I am comfortable talking to them, because in so many ways, I know that I am them, and they are me.

Chapter Eleven
The Ministry

When I was a child, first thinking about what I was going to do to help change the world, I believed I would go into the ministry. By the time I was eight years old, in my mind my future was set. In fact, I grew up almost expected to go into the ministry.

As I've said, my grandfather was in the ministry, and two of my uncles were also ministers, and in a few years my older brother LeRoy would enter seminary, and I was going to follow in their footsteps. Some of my earliest memorable thoughts were that I wanted to change the world, and as I grew, I thought being in the ministry may be the way to do that.

I was a church kid, and spent a lot of time in and around church. But I think my goal to be a minister had more to do with a calling. By the time I was eleven or twelve, I understood "the calling," the concept that you are personally chosen to do a certain kind of work. I understood that "calling," and I sensed it strongly.

I grew up at a time when religion played an important role in small town America. Even though the town I grew up in was only about a mile square, it had eight or nine churches. Every other block or so, there was a church. There was an abundance of Lutheran churches, a United Brethren church, a Catholic church, and a Baptist church. The public school even let all of its students out of class every Tuesday afternoon so they could all walk to their individual churches to attend "Tuesday School" for religious instruction. (Try that today.)

I was extremely religious in my thinking. I remember having to knowingly fail every test in science class that asked how long humans had been on Earth. At that time, according to the church

I was raised in, the answer was about 6,000 years. The science teacher in school did not agree.

I was not a perfect child, but being a church kid I probably thought more about spiritual things and helping others than some of my friends, but I was just a kid. Doing kid things and trying to get life right.

As I grew older, closer to the time I was to cast the die of my life forever by going to seminary, becoming ordained, and becoming the pastor of a church, I began to think that my calling might not be for the ministry itself, but for something else. Something close to the ministry, but not necessarily working in a single church with a single congregation. After thinking a lot about this, I announced to my parents that I was not going to follow my lifelong dream of becoming a minister. I remember telling them that I wanted "to reach more than a hundred and forty-five communicant members, mostly on church holidays." I wanted to open the doors wider—and invite *everyone* in. My parents were disappointed at first, but in time, they understood.

It was the right decision. Many of my audiences today look like international UNICEF conventions—people from every country and faith fill those audiences. If I had gone into the ministry in the narrower sense of the word, I would have never reached most of the people I've been able to reach.

In all the time I have been speaking to a more world-wide audience, there have only been a few people who, without understanding how the brain gets programmed, have questioned the fact that I recommend that they "believe in themselves." By saying that, however, I never imply that they shouldn't believe in the higher spirit of their faith; they should believe whatever they choose. The evidence for the programming process of the brain— how you wire your brain with your thoughts—is not a philosophical or a theological argument; it is just stating the facts of how the neural programming process of the brain works.

One could summarize my first book, *What to Say When You Talk to Your Self,* by the scriptural passage from Romans 12:2, ". . . *be transformed by the renewing of your mind."* Even though that book is not about religion, and I focused on neuroscience rather than on spirituality, the pages of the book say in a life-changing scientific way exactly that: be transformed by the renewing of your mind.

What is predominant among the people who have read my books or attended my seminars, is how incredibly all-encompassing my message has been. Truth speaks to all people who seek truth.

As one example of this, I was invited to fly to Salt Lake City to meet with a board of leaders of The Church of Jesus Christ of Latter-Day Saints, the Mormon Church. When I sat at the meeting table with the distinguished leaders who were present, I saw that, in front of them, each had a copy of my book *What to Say When You Talk to Your Self,* and all of their copies had been heavily annotated and highlighted.

They began the meeting by reading relevant passages from the Doctrine and Covenants, an important part of the teaching of the Mormon Church. The group's leader then told me that it was their belief to find truth wherever truth existed, no matter where it came from. Then, for more than two hours, they asked good questions about what I had written—clearly wanting to understand it completely. I left the meeting with a great level of respect for those leaders.

Over the years, people of every kind of faith would see the same thing: truth is truth; this is how the brain works. I have been blessed that my message has been understood and taught by people of all faiths. To some, the workings of the brain are a miracle, and a clear gift from the Creator. To others, less spiritually inclined, it's all science. To my mind, in the end they are one and the same.

65

My goal in my work with self-talk has always been to reach as many people as possible. I've been fortunate that my books have been translated into many languages and published in more than seventy countries during the years I've been writing.

Just recently, I agreed to the publication of editions of *What to Say When You Talk to Your Self* in even more languages—in Arabic in the Middle East, in six languages in India, in traditional Chinese, in Korean, in Vietnamese, in Turkish, and in Russian—that would take the message to people around the world that I wasn't previously reaching.

As I reviewed these requests from the various publishers in the different countries, I could not help but think about how many of the people who would read my words were people who had lived under the yoke of tyranny, and my own words of unlimited freedom—freedom of thought, freedom of opportunity and freedom to achieve as individuals—were finally being welcomed into their lives and into their world.

I have found that when speaking in person, my audiences for many years have been filled with every color, every faith, every political direction, and every lifestyle. And the telling point of all of this—believing in people no matter who they are, where they came from, or what they believe—is when you meet them and talk to them in person.

In every seminar or audience where I can, I set aside time to meet with people, one-on-one—not just to shake their hand, but to focus on them individually, and talk to them as though they were the only other person in the world. In *my* mind, when I'm talking to them, they are.

After one seminar, an elderly lady, small, frail, and dignified, stood in line, waiting to talk to me. People were asking to have books signed, or just wanted to talk. When her turn finally came, the elderly lady clutched my hand, very hard, and held on to it, and would not let it go. As she held my hand, her eyes filled with tears.

She told me her name was Greta, and then she just stood there for very long moments, looking at me. And then she said, "I'm here because my husband passed away three years ago, when he was eighty-five. When he was gone, I didn't know what to do, and I couldn't imagine going on without him. Then someone gave me your book, and I read it. And it gave my life back to me. It let me know I could go on. And I came here today to thank you."

Greta had gotten the message of the book, and it had given her hope and a way to deal with the loss she was going through. Her tears weren't tears of sadness; they were tears of joy.

It has been in those personal touches, meeting the real people from everywhere, looking at them, seeing each other eye-to-eye, listening to their stories, giving and getting thousands of hugs, caring about them individually, that I came to know the people with whom I share this planet. They come from every possible walk of life. They are rich and poor, confident and struggling, certain and seeking. In one moment, I am talking to a woman who has lost her husband. Moments later I am meeting a young family that is learning about self-talk for the first time.

When language is a barrier, I just pause, wait, let the words come out, and in time they do. People from places I have never been, and who drove or flew long distances to get there, stand in front of me, often nervous, and look cautiously to my eyes to see if I really see them. And I always see them. I know them. I understand more than the words they struggle to say. But in the end, we not only communicate, we get each other's message: *I'm so glad to know you. I love you too.*

I believe that none of those connections with those people would have happened if I had stayed on my youthful path to become a minister in the church. If I had stayed on that path, I know I would have been a good minister. I would have shepherded my flock of a few hundred parishioners, taught them from the pulpit, and counseled them in their daily lives. But I

67

probably would never have reached people in China or Russia or India or Saudi Arabia.

And I would never have met Greta, who looked at me—eyes watering with tears, and clutching my hand, needing for me to know—and wouldn't let go.

I believe that when it gets down to it, the true calling of life is what we can do to help others in whatever way we can. From the time I was a very young child, raised in a religious home, dedicated to going into the "ministry," I stayed on that path. I may not have followed my grandfather and my uncles into their kind of ministry, but I found my own. And if I am ever asked in Heaven if I did anything well, I will tell them about Greta, and helping her when she thought she could not go on.

What I learned:

This lesson became clear to me when I spoke to my first audience, and it became more pronounced the more often I spoke: It's not the robe we wear or the banner above the door—it is the words we speak and the message we share that count. I learned that my respect for my grandfather, and the "ministers" in my life, did not emanate from the church that ordained them; it came from the work they were doing and the message they were sharing. Were they still living today, I know that each of them would agree.

Chapter Twelve
The Three Questions

I cannot begin to tell you how many people have asked me what put me on the path I followed in my life. Especially at seminars or speaking events when there is a question and answer session, someone will almost always ask me why I chose to do what I chose to do.

When I'm asked that question, I seldom have enough time to give a proper answer. I usually answer by saying, with sincerity, "It wasn't luck," or "I had a plan to follow."

What I usually don't have the time to express is that the path I followed—that is, writing and speaking and presenting the life-changing concept of self-talk to the world—did not happen by accident. It actually happened because of three questions I asked myself very early in my life. It was a simple idea, but it had major results.

I was in my teens when the idea of "the three questions" came to me. I don't know where the idea came from exactly; it could have been while I was daydreaming one Sunday during church, or something I dreamed one night. I don't think the idea came to me at school, because I can't remember any really important idea ever coming to me at school. But as soon as I began to think about the idea of the three questions, I was intrigued by it.

The idea was that if I could answer the three most important questions I could ever ask myself about my direction in life, then I would have a better idea of both my purpose in life, and the path I should follow. Big thoughts for a teenaged kid maybe, but it tied into my dream of wanting to change the world, and once the idea of the three questions came to me, I never let it go.

When I was growing up, my father wouldn't allow a television set in the house (he said that television was "a thief that sat in the corner of the room and stole your dreams"), and listening to rock and roll on the radio was equally forbidden in our household, so that opened up a lot of brain space for thinking about any thought that came along. I think I was lucky that one of those thoughts was the idea of "the three questions."

The fascinating thing about the three questions was that *I didn't know what they were*. So it wasn't as if I had given myself a quiz, and all I had to do was answer some questions. My idea was that I would start by *not knowing the questions*. Then, after I had successfully found out what the *questions* were, I would then have to find the *answers*. (I learned later, that in doing this I was wading, unknowingly, in Zen waters.)

To give you an accurate feel for what the experience was like, as you read the chapter at this point, transport yourself back to the person you were at about sixteen or seventeen years old. In our teenage years, most of us know very little about *anything*. At least *I* didn't. But thinking as you thought at that age, what *three* questions would you have asked yourself that would guide you on the best possible course on your path through life?

I don't know how you feel about doing that, but for some reason, at the time, I was drawn to the idea, and I thought about it a lot.

The first task was to figure out what the three questions were. I'm not certain how long it took me to find the exact three questions I was looking for, but at that time in my life, still spending endless hours working in the farm fields, time wasn't an issue; I had plenty of it.

Also, the solitude I had working in the fields gave me a clarity that I don't think I would have found if I had lived as a teenager in the city. In the fields, in the quiet, endless countryside, I saw life differently. From the sun rising, filtering its early light through the rainbow prism of colors in the beads of dew on each blade of grass, to traveling its long, slow journey across the sky, measuring the day, hour by hour by its path, to the last gleam of golden light before the fields around me rested for the night, I had endless hours to think about my three questions.

So instead of dreading the time I spent alone, I looked forward to it: more time to think, more time to talk to myself, more time to find the right questions and get them so clear that I would be able to find good, clear answers.

(Interestingly, years later, in the 1970's, when I would begin my work in the unexplored profession of life coaching, I believed—correctly—that *perfect* life coaching would be the coach asking the clients exactly the right questions, and allowing the clients to find the answers within themselves. Long before there were life coaches, by asking myself the three most important questions early in my own life, I was doing essentially what I would be doing for my clients, when I was developing my concept of life coaching, twenty years later.)

Although I don't remember exactly how long the search for the three questions took, I know that I went through dozens of questions before I found the right ones. When I thought about the questions that came to me, and when I studied them, turning them over in my mind, I intuitively knew whether or not *this* one or *that* one was a question that would be one of the special questions that would lead me through the next, important years of my life.

Even at the time, I knew how important the questions would be. And I knew that if I kept looking, I would find them. So that's what I did; I kept looking.

And finally, because I stayed with it, in time, *I had them*. All three of my questions. As I found each of them, I wrote them down. And when I finally saw them listed together, neatly, in clear, open handwriting in my journal, one below the other, I remember thinking how incredibly, unbelievably simple my final three questions were. Almost too simple for *anyone* to take seriously—unless they understood.

My final three questions were:

What?
How?
When?

How simple they were! But what power they held. In those three questions, the path to finding my direction in life became clear to me.

What was it I would choose to do?
How would I make it happen?
When would I begin, and bring it to life in my life?

From that time forward, as I grew from my teens into my twenties, I kept those three questions with me. Not only were they never far from my mind, they proved to be the creative foundation beneath most of the life-affecting decisions I would make for years to come.

I also understood right from the start, that it wasn't about how long it would take me to find the *answers* to the questions—taking the time to find the *right* answers would hold the key to my future.

(My personal opinion on this is: It doesn't matter how long it has taken you to get to where you are today. If you want to ask yourself the same questions that I asked myself, and if you're still breathing, you can still answer the questions with your own answers.)

I knew that it made no difference if it took me months or even years to answer each of the questions. My deal with myself was: it wasn't about the time it would take; it was about getting this life *right*—no matter how long it took—so that I would end up doing what I came here to do.

I learned early on that if you ask a question often enough, and are willing to listen for the answer, the answer will always show up. As soon as I began to ask the first question of myself—the *What* question—my brain started searching for the answer.

Though at the time it may have seemed to me that my quest to find my path took a long time, the highlights of those years can be best told in a few, short paragraphs that summarize my search for the answers to the three questions:

When the idea of "positive self-talk," and how a person's thoughts can wire his or her brain in a new, positive way, came into my life, it was clear that *that* was the answer to the question of "*What*" I wanted to do with my life.

I wanted to help people, and with the discovery of self-talk I had a way to do that. The message of positive self-talk was *exactly* the "*What*" I had been looking for. It was new, it was important, it was based on solid science, and when practiced, it changed lives.

The second question—*How?*—helped me get ready for the task. It was the *How* question that got me to go back to school as an adult. It was the *How* question that got me to seek out career opportunities that would train me with the right skills. And it was the "*How*" that got me to explore how I would get my message out to the world, and lay out the blueprint for a career in writing and speaking—so I could present my ideas effectively.

The third question—*When?*—told me when it was time to make my goal happen. It was that question that got me to begin writing self-talk scripts for audio recordings that I could share with everyone, and not long after, to begin speaking publicly, appearing on television, and writing my first book on the subject. The "*When*" had finally become "*Now.*"

From that time forward, I stayed on the course that my three questions had set into motion.

I have been surprised from time to time, when I've stopped to take stock of my life to see how I was doing, that I was still following exactly what those three questions had first defined.

While I may never feel that I'm doing enough, I take consolation in the fact that I'm still working at it. And it continues to be an incredible reason to get up each morning. It also continues to keep me focused, and reminds me why I'm here.

I'm not sure what my life would have looked like, or what I would have done had I not asked myself those three questions. (What if I had come up with three completely different questions, and three completely different answers than the ones I ended up following?)

It doesn't mean that I reached every goal I set, or that I did everything right. I didn't. I missed a lot of goals, and I made mistakes that I cower to think of, on the way to working out the *What*, the *How*, and the *When* of the purpose of my own life. But I cannot even imagine what the same passing years would have looked like had I not had a direction and a plan to follow along the way.

Looking at it now, I'm quite certain that if I had not worked to find and follow the answers to the three questions, you would not be reading this book right now. You would be doing something else. And this book, and the ideas that preceded it, would never have been.

What I learned:
The entire process of searching for the three questions and their answers taught me the value of having a life map to follow. But even more important than that was what following the path of the three questions taught me about taking responsibility for myself. I was designing my life around those questions without relying on someone *else* to tell me what I should do. Instead of asking for permission for how I should live my life—I was figuring

it out for myself; it was my life, my heartbeats, my thoughts, my breaths, my footsteps and my future. What happened would be up to me, and the choices I made.

That's more important today than ever, because we are living at a time when our society is creating a culture of victimhood, and all too many people are learning to blame others for their own mistakes or for what happens in their lives—instead of taking responsibility for themselves. They learn to believe they are victims, which is sad, because there is neither courage nor success in victimhood.

What I found in the three questions—and their answers—was a plan. It was a future that would not be up to anyone else to make it happen; my life, and the results of what I did with it, would be up to me.

Although, as I was to learn, I would sometimes have unexpected help along the way—as we will see in the following chapter.

Chapter Thirteen
The Bookstore

We usually understand most of the things that happen to us in our lives. But now and then something happens that can't easily be explained. For me, an unplanned visit to a bookstore was one of those experiences that defy an easy explanation. Here's what happened.

When I was in my twenties, I was traveling on business for the electronics/music company I worked for. This was several years before I had begun writing about self-talk and personal growth. On this occasion, I had flown into Tampa, Florida, arriving late on a Thursday evening so I would be there in time for a meeting that had been scheduled for 9:00 a.m. Friday morning.

After I had picked up my rental car at the airport and checked in at my hotel that evening, I decided I would drive to the location of the next day's meeting and check it out, so I would know how to get there and I would be certain to be on time. So the night before, I found the address, which was located in a large shopping center area, about eight in the evening.

I made sure I knew exactly where to go for the meeting the next morning, and prepared to return to my hotel. Although it was late and getting dark, I noticed a small strip of stores bordering the large parking area, and one of them, a bookstore, had its lights on and looked like it was still open.

Being an avid reader, I loved bookstores, and I could easily spend an hour just browsing through the books. I was working for a good company, but what I earned wasn't enough for me to buy many books, and with a family to take care of, I was closely watching my expenses. But I could afford an occasional book.

On this particular evening, with nothing better to do, I pulled my rental car into a parking space in front of the bookstore, noticing that there were no other cars in the parking area. I hoped the store would still be open, and when I went to the door I found it wasn't locked, so I was in luck.

As soon as I entered the store I noticed the woman behind the small counter to the left of the entrance. Behind her was a doorway. The woman was an older woman, and very intelligent looking, with gray hair nicely worn to just above her shoulders. Every one of the wrinkles on her tanned face said "wisdom" and matched the look in her eyes as she welcomed me into the store.

Because the first words she said to me were so unexpected, I've always remembered them. She said, "Hello. Please come in. *We've been expecting you.*"

I turned to look behind me, to see if there was someone else following me in, but there wasn't anyone else there, so I realized the woman was talking to me.

I said "Hello" back, thinking the woman must have mistaken me for someone else. I said that I just happened to be in the area, and if they were still open, I would like to look around a little. I wasn't sure if I could afford to buy a book at that moment, but this was a bookstore, and browsing was what you got to do in bookstores. So overlooking her remark about being expected, I started toward the rows of bookshelves, deciding where I would search first.

Then, just as I turned toward one of the aisles, another woman appeared from the doorway behind the sales counter. This woman was also older; she had long gray hair and wore a colorful shawl.

With a kind smile, she also welcomed me to the store, and encouraged me to look around. She, too, said they had been

77

expecting me, and that I was right on time—as if they knew I would be arriving just when I did.

Then, oddly, she asked me to verify my birthday, which I politely did. She seemed pleased that it was the date she had already known it to be, and it affirmed to her that I was indeed the person they had been expecting.

It was a "Twilight Zone" experience. I had arrived at the bookstore on a whim, but, yet, they were expecting me—and they knew the date of my birthday! Completely confused, and not knowing exactly how to deal with this unusual situation, I turned dumbly down the first aisle and started looking at the books on the shelves.

I had just gotten to the back of the first row of bookshelves when I realized the first older woman with the wisdom wrinkles had followed me, and she was now taking a book off a top shelf. After she did, she handed it to me and said, "Here. You'll like this one. This is one you're going to need."

I took the book, not sure what to say, but she didn't give me the chance to say anything. Selecting a second book, this one from a lower shelf, she said, "This is another one you'll need," and held it out for me to take. Within a few minutes, the older lady had handed me another book, commenting on its importance to me, and then another book, and then another.

At the time, as I went through the shelves of books, with the woman carefully selecting one book from one shelf, and another book from another shelf, my mind was racing, completely uncertain as to what was going on. Instead of me casually browsing through the books in a bookstore that I had happened upon by complete accident in a place I had never been—and had no intention of visiting—one of the two older ladies was carefully selecting books from the shelves, telling me with each of them that *this* was a book I would *need*. It made no sense to me at all.

Finally, when I had twelve books stacked in my arms, I decided I needed to make my exit, put the stack of books on the counter, thank the two ladies for their time, and get the heck out of there.

So I turned up an aisle, went up to the front counter, and said my exit speech. I thought it was brilliant, and I remember it, word for word. I thought that what had been foisted upon me was an amazing selling technique. So I said, "If I could only afford one of these books, which one would you recommend?" knowing that if I said this, I could buy a single book, even if I couldn't really afford it, pay the ransom, and escape.

What happened next was amazing. Not only was I not prepared for it, but neither have I ever been able to explain it, in any practical way.

What happened next was that the woman said to me, *"Oh, you can't buy these books. These books are for you. You'll need them for what you're here to do."*

Still confused and now stunned, I ended up negotiating with the two elegant, gray-haired ladies to reduce the number of books from twelve down to eight. I then tried to pay for at least one of the books, but the ladies wouldn't accept any payment.

With the two women smiling in wisdom and kindness, I ended up carrying eight, expensive, hardcover books out of the bookstore, and putting them carefully in the passenger seat in my car. I drove back to my hotel, trying to make sense of what had just happened. As soon as I got to my hotel room, I called my wife and said, "You'll never believe what just happened to me," and told her the story while it was completely fresh in my mind. (I wanted someone else to be able to remember, in detail, what had just taken place.)

To this day, I have no practical explanation for what happened. I had visited the bookstore on a whim, I arrived without knowing I was going there, and I left the store with some of the most important books on personal growth that I would ever read. In the years following, as I went on to study and write about human behavior, and speak about it to audiences around the world, I often thought of my unusual bookstore experience.

If you are someone who believes that life is nothing more than chemical activity, and that there is no more to our lives than what we can measure in a laboratory, you will call my experience a psychological illusion or some form of aberration of coincidence. But if you see life as being greater than what we can measure in a laboratory or easily explain, you could see my bookstore experience as evidence that there is something to life that is beyond what we can touch or see. Whatever you think, I kept the books, and yes, they helped me on the path I was to follow in this lifetime.

As a curious footnote to this story, a second, but different experience occurred two or three years later that brought the bookstore vividly back to mind, and confirmed just how prescient life can be.

I was teaching an evening class on marketing at De Anza College in Cupertino, California. On my way to class one evening, I stopped to read the bulletin board that included posters and notices of upcoming events. One of the announcements said that a well-known paranormal researcher would be giving a talk on campus in the near future, and the public was invited.

I was raised with skepticism about psychic things, but I was interested in recent work that was being done in the area of the scientific testing of paranormal research, and I thought it might be interesting to attend the lecture. When I suggested this to my wife, who was a registered nurse with a background in science, she, too, thought it might be an interesting evening, and we decided to attend.

The lecture hall was one not unlike the one where I taught my own class, and when my wife and I arrived for the lecture, we chose to sit about halfway up in the center of the elevated seating area. By the time the program was ready to begin, there were a hundred or more people in the audience, so the lecture room was nicely filled with a good turnout.

The speaker took the podium on time, and talked for about forty-five minutes about how science is proving many areas of paranormal experience to be measurable, and that most of what we call psychic phenomena is starting to be shown as natural capabilities of the human mind, and not "psychic" at all. (At the time, the United States government was just beginning its "remote viewing" experiments at Stanford University, just a few miles from where my wife and I were attending the lecture.)

After a very informative lecture, the speaker said that he would demonstrate the capabilities of the human mind to "read" information he would gather from members of the audience. After two or three other attendees asked questions about things like getting messages from deceased loved ones, or other personal information, it seemed to me that the speaker was hitting things right on target, and he wasn't asking any leading questions or surfing for more information. He simply responded to each question asked, in a very straightforward, almost clinical way.

My wife, who was sitting next to me, had been considering a job change, from working as a registered nurse at one hospital to a nursing position at another location, and I thought that asking a question about her possible job change would be a safe, simple test of the speaker's claims. So while other people in the audience raised their hands to ask a question, I also raised mine.

The moment I raised my hand, the speaker ignored all of the others in the audience who were raising their hands, stopped, raised his own hands, motioning for everyone to put their hands down, and stood patiently on the stage while the room became silent.

When everything was still, the speaker gestured up to me, paused for a long, thoughtful moment, and said: "You were going to ask me a question about a nurse. I would assume that would be the lady sitting next to you."

He then stopped, and went into what looked like deep thought for another long moment, and then looked up again, directly at me. He said, "*I* should be up *there*, sitting in the audience, and *you* should be down *here*, answering questions. *And one day, you will be.*"

And then the speaker looked away from me, turned to the rest of the audience, and said, "Next question."

I turned to my wife, who was just as surprised as I was. He had been exactly right. The question in my mind when I raised my hand did have to do with a nurse, and she was the person sitting next to me. But having said that, he ignored the question I was going to ask, and gave me an entirely different message.

If I had not experienced the earlier, unexplained visit with the bookstore ladies, attending an evening event with a paranormal researcher on a college campus would probably have come and gone almost unnoticed, with little more than lingering curiosity. But both of them happened, and they stayed in my mind.

Not only did the two unexplained experiences suggest to me that life has more mysteries within it than we might know, but they proved to be uncannily correct about what was to come, and what I was about to do with the rest of my life.

What I learned:

I've gotten used to things happening that are unusual or impossible to explain away. Even with all we know, there are more things we *don't* understand, than things that we *do*, and experiences like the two I've mentioned here taught me to keep an open mind.

Shakespeare's Hamlet was correct when he said, *"There are more things in Heaven and Earth, Horatio, than are dreamt of in your philosophy."*

Chapter Fourteen
The Journey Begins

I believe that the path I've taken through this life has not been an accidental one. But to find out how I got from being a boy in a wheat field to an author in the self-help field, the answer can best be found in what I did in my career path *before* I wrote my first book.

Here is the beginning of my journey:

After leaving my home and the farmlands forever behind me, I spent time in Cuba, as a Spanish/English interpreter (which I will tell you about in a later chapter). When I returned to the United States, I was just twenty years old, a few months short of my twenty-first birthday.

I came home to a young wife and our one-year-old son Anthony. We moved into a small, upstairs garage apartment behind my parents-in-law's home, and I started looking for work. I wanted to go back to school, but I knew that I would have to wait until I could find a job so I could take care of my family.

While I was in Cuba, I had purchased a foreign tape recorder, the early kind with seven inch reels of tape to record and play music. After I returned to the United States, I discovered that the tape recorder I had purchased would not work on American electrical current, so I took it to a music and electronics store to have it converted.

I visited that store frequently while I was waiting for the repair, and I got to know the owner of the store. He was an older gentleman who had a doctorate in music, and along with owning the music store, he was also the distinguished conductor of our city's symphony orchestra.

Each time I visited his store, it became more apparent to me that this fine gentleman was probably a better symphony conductor than he was an electronic equipment store owner. After I had waited for two or three weeks for my tape recorder to be converted, and it still wasn't, and after I had visited his store several times to check on the progress, on one visit an idea came to me.

"You should hire me," I said, out of the blue, "to help you run your business."

I may have surprised him by offering to go to work for him, but he decided to hire me. Then, after a few months of working for him, I surprised him again by suggesting that he sell his business to me.

Apparently the fact that I was barely out of my teens and knew absolutely *nothing* about running a business did not occur to me at the time. Nor must it have occurred to the proprietor of the music/electronics store, because a few weeks later, he agreed to sell me his business.

The transaction actually had to wait a while, until I reached my twenty-first birthday, so I could sign legal documents. Then, the music doctor, along with his wife and an attorney, gathered at the local bank, and the bank vice president officially presented me with the loan papers to sign. I signed them, and I bought my first business.

For the time being, I knew that I didn't have to keep looking for work; I could now hire myself.

I managed the music electronics business for a year, and then I decided it was time to expand. A few months later I opened a second store in a shopping mall in another city an hour and a half away.

To promote my music store business, the manager of the local classical music FM radio station was doing his best to interest me in advertising on his radio station. It made sense; people who listen to classical music would be the same people who would purchase the high-quality stereo music amplifiers, turntables, and speakers I was selling in my stores.

Instead of having to pay full-price for the advertising time on the classical music station, I told the station manager that I had an idea: I would produce and host a two-hour classical music program every week-day night on his station—thus lowering his operating costs because he wouldn't have to hire a classical music host during that all-important, evening, classical music listening time slot.

He agreed. I don't think either he or I ever mentioned in our conversation that I had never done a radio show, and that I had absolutely no experience in doing one.

But in spite of my lack of experience, my venture into radio was a success. I had grown up listening to classical music, I knew a lot about it, and I had a new, fresh take on almost everything from Beethoven to Bartok. I would record my nightly classical music program during the day, on tape, and drive it out to the radio station, which was miles out in the country, each night.

But while the radio show was a success, having to manage a business successfully every day was more difficult.

I had not yet, at this time, discovered what my real direction in life was to be, but I finally decided it was not managing music stores; I knew I needed to find something beyond that. I had gotten into business on the spur of the moment, with absolutely no goal or plan in mind, and I was beginning to realize that that is *not* how you create a life that works.

So after doing well with one of my two music stores, and not well with the other one, after a couple of years, I sold one of them and closed the other, and left with nothing more than my first experience in business.

Throughout this time I felt that there was a greater purpose to my life than "*this.*" I was still very much aware of the fact that I had wanted to change the world, and now I was letting myself down; I wasn't coming anywhere *close* to doing something that would change the world, let alone helping anyone. And even though I was still very young, I thought maybe life was passing me by, and I was missing out on my chance to make a difference.

At this time, I hadn't yet found the answers to my three questions about what I would do with my life. I didn't know what my real purpose was, but I was sure there was one. I was confident enough to believe that I could open any door I wanted to—all I had to do was to know the right door to open and exercise the creativity I had been trained to use as a youth—and I believed that anything was possible, *if I could just figure out what it was.*

By this time I was the ripe old age of twenty-three. I had been a foreign language interpreter, owned two businesses, hosted a successful classical music radio show, and was just beginning to understand that even though the whole world was in front of me, I had no clear course of direction set for my life.

I had learned that I could succeed; I had also learned that I could fail—and I had learned that I had no idea where I was going.

My family and I were living in Memphis, Tennessee, when my second son, Gregory, was born. I had taken a job in Memphis working for another electronics/music store.

(The store I worked at was directly across the street from Sun Recording Studios where Elvis Presley, Jerry Lee Lewis, Johnny Cash, and Roy Orbison recorded their first hits. I was there, in Memphis, just six blocks from Martin Luther King when he was shot, and I happened to record a CB radio transmission that sounded like it was a visual sighting on the getaway car. The police came and got my recording and I never saw it again.)

In my own life, my family was growing and I decided I had to get serious about the future. I didn't know yet what that future would be, but I was starting to realize that I was writing the script myself—and if I was, it was up to me to get it right. No more instant, life-changing decisions without thinking them through; no more hoping or waiting for life to work itself out.

I decided that the first step would be to get into a position that would help me learn more about the larger world of business, along with offering me the opportunity to go back to school. It wasn't a complete picture, but it was the beginning of a plan.

As a first step I chose to go to work for a large, international electronics and music corporation as a junior executive-in-training. I ended up spending several years with that company, which moved me from Memphis to Chicago, and then to California.

I had not forgotten the three questions I had believed would help my find the right path to follow in my life, and it was during the time I was working in the corporate environment that I began to once again focus on those three questions and identify what my real goal was—and I was certain that it had to do with helping people in a positive way.

I began to study what I would have to do to accomplish my goal of helping people change their lives. The first thing I decided to do was go back to school at night, so I could work on my degree. Over the next several years I would continue working, while at the same time, taking more classes.

There were times when I was taking a full class load of college courses at night, while I was so busy with my corporate job that I would get off an airplane in Chicago, where I was living at the time, hand my completed course assignments to my secretary, and she would drive them out to the college while I was getting on another airplane to fly to California for another business meeting.

Because I was busy, but dedicated to doing well with my classwork, I asked to meet with each of my college instructors. At each of those meetings I explained that I was a very serious student, and I had a goal to make nothing less than a 4.0 or "A" grade, and I made a deal with each of them: If there was something I was not doing, that I should be doing to reach my goal, they would tell me. And in turn, if there was something *they* should be doing but weren't doing, as my instructors, *I* would tell *them*. That was the deal, and it must have helped because I never received less than a 4.0. That was my goal.

The high grade level wasn't important because I needed it on a resume; it was important because I knew that receiving high grades would keep me motivated. And when you're getting out of your last class at ten at night, in the middle of winter, and making your way across a frozen parking lot, trying not to slip or fall on the ice, and then driving home in a blinding snowstorm, you have to be motivated to keep doing it.

(On one occasion, each of the students was required to do an oral report on consumer protection, and what corporations should do to be compliant with federal regulations. I didn't have time to research or write a lengthy report, so I showed up at class and when it was my time to give my report I went to the front of the room, stood behind the podium, and pushed the "play" button on a cassette player I had brought with me.

For the next twenty minutes the instructor and the class listened, with great attention, to a one-on-one "live" interview I had taped earlier that day with the director of the Good Housekeeping Seal of Approval, one of the most recognized consumer conscious brands in the country.

I had called their director, and when I reached him I told him I needed to do an interview for my class; he was thrilled to do it. The class and the instructor *loved* it. Standing ovation. And I got a 4.0 on my report.)

It was during this time, with me living in the business world, that I started carefully evaluating everything I was doing. I liked working in the corporate environment and the security it offered. Plus, it was making it possible to continue going to school, and also paying for the formal education I needed to acquire. But as secure and supportive as it was, there were two reasons why I decided that I would have to leave the comfortable world of corporate life:

The first was that I recognized I could never reach my goal of helping people the way I wanted to, while I was working within the confines of a corporation. Appropriately, while I was working for the corporation, my work time had to be devoted to the *company's* goals, not *mine*.

The second reason I decided I had to leave corporate life was that I wanted to gain first-hand experience in the area of *"personal growth,"* a field I had decided would be instrumental in helping me help others.

So after several years of living in the corporate cocoon, I decided to leave that world behind me and strike out on my own. It was a big decision, but this time it was not a spur-of-the-moment decision; it was completely thought through, and it was part of a plan.

I remember how my work associates, "lifers" in the corporate world, advised me against leaving it. *All* of my friends thought I should stay; they all thought leaving was just too "risky." (This was, perhaps, my first lesson in the benefits of not living your life based on the opinions of others.)

But I had thought it through. I knew if I stayed where I was, in my safe, comfortable, successful, always-on-the-way-up job, the corporate world could end up being my whole *life*—and I had decided my life was about more than that. Staying safe would use up my time and my energies and keep me from focusing on what I really wanted to do most.

90

Because of my long-time interest in personal motivation, I was very skilled in motivational marketing—that was the area of work I was doing for the corporation that employed me.

But an idea had come to me and it wouldn't let go. I reasoned that *if the right marketing campaign could convince someone to get up off the sofa, while watching his favorite ball game on television on a Saturday afternoon, and get that person to go out and buy something he didn't need, or didn't even know he wanted—if motivational marketing could do that, why not use those same methods to sell people on themselves—instead of on some unnecessary product?* (If you could "program" someone's brain to buy a product, why couldn't you also program someone's brain to be more successful, or be more organized, or have better relationships, as an example?)

What if that idea held within it an answer to my search for a way to help people improve their lives? It was an idea I would continue to pursue. And it was an idea that would be the beginning of the turning point in my life.

By the time I left my corporate position, I was prepared for what I would do next; I had a plan, and as part of that plan, I had already taken steps to open my own consulting company. As a consultant, I could pick and choose my clients, and I would also have the freedom I would need to work on my personal goal. My first step was to find clients who worked in the personal growth field, the field I was drawn to and wanted to learn.

One of my first opportunities was a company that produced self-improvement audio cassette programs—exactly the kind of "success company" I wanted to work with.

When I agreed to work with this company, I was given an office and a desk, and I stayed with them for almost two years. But after that, I knew it was time to go to the next step, and not stay in one place.

What is unique and especially interesting about my moving on was what happened on the last day I was with that company. It was a Saturday. The business offices were closed for the weekend, and I had gone back to my office a final time to pick up my personal belongings.

I was there by myself, putting my things into a cardboard box, when I heard a knock on the front door of the building. I wondered who that could be. The place was closed, but the knocking continued, so I made my way through the darkened outer offices to the front door, and opened it.

Standing outside the door was a well-dressed, refined-looking, silver-haired man. He introduced himself and asked if he could come in. I had never met him, but I knew who he was; he was a legend in the personal growth field. He was the founder and CEO of the world's largest motivational training company, a top-tier "success company." If there was one person in the personal achievement industry that I would like to know, it would be him.

I invited him to my office where the cardboard box of my personal things was sitting open on top of my desk, and invited him to have a seat.

We exchanged pleasantries and talked for a couple of minutes. He told me he just happened to be in the city, and on a whim had decided to drop in. And then, looking at the box of files, knickknacks and framed photographs sitting on the top of my desk, he politely asked, "What are you doing?"

"I'm cleaning out my desk," I said. "I'm a consultant, and I've been working with this company for the past two years, and I'm in the process of leaving."

"What kind of consulting do you do?" he asked.

"I solve marketing problems and come up with creative solutions," I told him. "My focus is companies in the personal growth industry."

"Why are you leaving this company?" he asked.

"I've completed my work here," I said. "It's time to move on."

Without another word, no more conversation, the gentleman stood up, handed me his business card, and said, "On Monday morning my secretary will send you an airline ticket to fly to Texas to meet with me and my management staff. Would you be willing to do that?"

I said that I would; we talked pleasantly for a few more minutes, and the gentleman left.

"How amazing is that?" I thought. I was cleaning out my desk, ready to move on in my quest to reach my goal of helping people change their lives, and the president of the world's leading success motivation training company had knocked on the door on a Saturday, completely unannounced, talked with me for a few minutes, and then told me I would receive an airline ticket to visit him at his company.

My decision to leave corporate life and strike out on my own as a consultant was working, in the most positive way. I flew to Texas and visited the motivation company, and the CEO of the company was true to his word. When I arrived, I was ushered into a meeting room with a large boardroom table with ten or twelve company managers seated around it. The CEO introduced me to the group by saying, "This is the kind of person we need helping us."

Later, after we had all gotten acquainted and had a chance to talk, the CEO asked his management team to vote on whether they should hire me as a consultant. When the vote was taken, the team agreed, and I was hired. It was a victory. With an introduction like the CEO had given me, I couldn't lose.

Two weeks later, I was spending so much of my time working with them, that I rented a condo in their city, to be near their offices.

My primary goal, the one I was actively working on, was to get to a place in my life where I could help people improve their lives.

My two biggest client/employers since leaving the corporate world were both leaders in the personal growth industry; I was on the right track.

My next major client was one of the top companies in sales training and personal achievement. This organization, located in Scottsdale, Arizona, was also an industry leader, and once again I found myself working with a "success company," my third one in a row.

Because I had been successful in finding consulting clients who, while I was helping them, gave me the opportunity to gain a valuable education in the personal growth field—in a period of just a few short years—I understood that field from every side. I had done good work for each of those companies, but because of my tenure with each of them, I was also able to learn the world of personal growth from the inside out.

By the time my consulting contract with the third personal growth company was coming to a close, I was finally ready to begin making my own goal a reality.

It was at that time, during the closing months of working with the third personal growth company as my client, that I began writing the first library of self-talk audio programs—the concept that would throw the doors to my goal wide open, and virtually change the rest of my life.

What I learned:

When I review the steps I took to reach a place in my life where I could begin to turn my goal into reality, it's clear that what happened next was not a coincidence; it was a guided plan with a lot of help along the way. In the process, I learned that goals have power, and clear, positive intentions attract good results.

I also learned that there is no greater earthly force than determination.

If you have any reasonable goal, and a plan to reach it, and if you take action and focus on that goal, stay practical and realistic but accept the possibility of your dream working, and absolutely refuse to stop, you will reach the goal.

Chapter Fifteen
The Message of Self-Talk

My first recognition of the idea of words having power began when I was a young boy sitting in church at my grandmother's funeral service. The minister was talking about my grandmother having a pure heart and a pure mind, and he quoted the Bible verse, *"As a man thinketh in his heart, so is he,"* from Proverbs 23:7.

Sitting there in church while the minister was delivering his eulogy, I remember thinking about those words over and over in my mind: *"How can that be? Thoughts aren't real. So how can a person be thoughts? How can thoughts be the person?"*

Those were my earliest questions on a subject that would end up creating my focus through much of my lifetime. The idea that thoughts could possibly *be the person*, kindled a fire in me, an inquiry into the workings of the human brain, and it was a fire that would never go out.

In time, I learned that the original message I got in church was correct—even scientifically correct: *As you think, so you become.* It may have first come into my brain from the wisdom of Biblical scripture, but the result of my interest in that simple message has been at the core of most of the work I've done in my life.

As a teenager, my brain always seemed to be busy figuring out things about people, especially why they did what they did. Why were some people always negative, or pessimistic, or quick to become angry? On the other hand, why were some other people always happy, positive, and optimistic? Or, why did some people get in the game, believe in themselves, take life on and win, while other people spent their entire lives sitting on the sidelines, never once believing they could have been a player?

Because I was interested in the subject of "thinking," while I was still a teenager in high school I read the book *The Power of Positive Thinking* by Dr. Norman Vincent Peale. None of the other teenagers I knew read self-help books, but I was interested in how people think, so I read it. That book, written from a spiritual perspective, strongly suggested that thinking positively could affect your success in life in just about anything.

But it was my father who made me think about the idea of attitude, and often put it to the test. If I looked like I was dejected or in a bad mood, he would encourage me to cheer up, to put a smile on my face. And as soon as I forced myself to cheer up or smile, I found that it usually worked, and I would start to feel better almost immediately. We've all experienced that.

Somewhere in my teenage years, I started to wonder *why* that worked. Why did telling yourself to cheer up actually make your attitude better? And you could *feel* it get better.

I also began to notice that people who had something major happen to them in their lives (such as heart surgery or the birth of a new baby), could change their attitude—and their lives—almost completely. I noticed that this was even true of people who were elderly; people whose attitudes had been unchanged for a lifetime could change their attitudes completely no matter what age they were.

Somewhere along the line, two avenues of thought converged in my mind. One was the three questions (*What? How? When?*) I had asked myself that would help me plan my future, and I had concluded that the answer to "*What?*" was that I wanted to devote my life to helping people.

Then, completely aside from that question, I found that I was deeply curious about how and why "attitude" *worked*. When those two thoughts came together, I began to think that the best way to help people would be to help them change their *attitudes*—about life and about themselves—from having low self-esteem, as an example, to beginning to see themselves in a positive way—as a way of life.

Most of the literature on the subject of attitude came from the field of psychology. Most of the literature on how to *use* attitudes to be more successful came from the field of self-help. But other than being told from psychological studies that attitude was affected by chemicals in the brain, and by self-help authors that you should change your attitude for the better, I wasn't finding anything that clearly defined how brain chemistry and personal optimism were tied together.

School textbooks at the time were still telling us that the adult human brain was essentially unchangeable; that we got only so many neurons, and we were stuck with what we got and how our DNA had arranged them. Once our brains were formed, our personalities were pretty much set. And that, many psychologists at the time still believed, also included our basic attitudes and outlook on life. By the time we made it to adulthood, most of *"who"* we were and *"how"* we were was cemented into place by the luck of the DNA draw—and the early conditioning we had gotten.

But then why could I, with a force of will, completely change my attitude? And why did some people go through a complete change in their attitudes and outlooks because of something happening in their lives? How could people change, *really* change, if their brains were no longer growing new neural connections and weren't *able* to change?

None of my early musings on the subject were necessarily ideas that would be accepted at that time in psychology classes in school; it would take several decades for that to change. And some of my ideas on attitude and the brain were completely inconsistent with tenets of neuroscience that were being taught at the time. (In a few years, that, too, would change).

My theory was that the brain itself was constantly growing and changing—creating new neural pathways—and that instead of being *set*, the brain was constantly rewiring itself.

And if my theory was correct, no matter what programs had been previously wired into our brains, we could change them. I thought that the popular argument over "nature vs. nurture" was the wrong argument. We would become not what nature gave us or how our early programs shaped our beliefs and attitudes; we would become what our own *thoughts* programmed our brains to believe—and *those thoughts* could be changed at any time.

The key was "*thoughts*."

Our brains were being physically wired by our thoughts.

The question then was, "What would be the best way to change our thoughts in order to change the wiring of our brain? What would be the best way to change the *thoughts* that were wiring our brains every day of our lives?"

As it happened, I was to find the answer in an experience from my own life. Because I had been a Spanish/English language interpreter, I knew that the very best way to learn a *new* language was to live in an environment in which only that language is spoken. That's language learning by "immersion," and it's very effective. But if you couldn't be in an immersive environment, you could also learn the language by listening to it repeatedly on audio recordings—which was also an effective way to learn a new language.

This experience came back to me when I was searching for the best way to rewire the brain with new thoughts. It was clear that learning a new language was, in fact, wiring that new language into new neural pathways in the brain.

I deduced that most attitudes are actually neural pathways that have been wired into the brain, and that you could conceivably wire in brand-new attitudes in exactly the same way that you would wire in a new language—by listening to it. (That's also how children first learn language, by repeatedly listening to it.)

And then, finally, I had it! *The key to changing programs was repetition! Repetition, repetition, repetition.*

To test my theory, I wrote specific phrases that were designed to create specific attitudes (*I believe in myself, I can do this, I'm always on time, I care about others, I have good relationships,* etc.,) and recorded the phrases, in repeated sequences, on cassette tapes. That would be like talking to yourself, but, with *repetition*—and with that repetition, wiring your brain with new thoughts, new messages— *the basic expressions of a new language.*

Instead of saying things to yourself that could be negative or destructive, it would be saying things to yourself that would be positive and constructive.

And also like learning a new language, I predicted that with repeated listening to those repeated phrases, your brain would soon "learn" the new phrases. It would physically wire them in, and you would be able to think and speak the new "language"— create new attitudes—completely naturally; the new phrases and the resulting attitudes would become part of the wiring of your brain.

I called that process—and those new phrases—"*self-talk.*"

The concept worked. People who listened to recorded self-talk phrases began to change their internal language. They began to think differently—based on the new, more positive messages they were listening to each day—and they began to notice differences in their thoughts and attitudes. (As an example, in an early test, I found that salespeople could increase their sales by listening to repeated self-talk phrases about closing sales.)

I began to realize that by mirroring language learning, I had found a way to change a person's mental language—their attitudes—and, in turn, change habits that had been working against them for years.

As exciting as it was to me, my "breakthrough" in personal growth was not without its detractors. By this time in my career, I knew a lot of people in the personal growth field, and some of them didn't immediately accept my new concept of self-talk. One of them, a well-known author and speaker, told me that self-talk could not possibly work; "It's too *simple*," he said. My response to him was, "It has to be simple. When it comes to rewiring the brain, if it isn't simple, it will not work." (If you ask people to do too much to make a change, they won't do it—their old programs will stop them.)

One executive of a leading personal growth audio company told me, "We don't need self-talk; we need to go back to the old way of doing it." He was defending his business model, which was "learn by having experts tell you what to do." He had missed the point. I wasn't suggesting you should stop learning from experts. I was working at a different level of brain-changing. With the right self-talk getting your mind right, your brain would be more receptive, and *all* learning would be more effective.

There were also people in the field of psychology who typically threw all new personal growth concepts into the trash-bin of "pseudoscience." They were convinced that if a concept hadn't been around for at least several decades, and been blessed by Freud or someone else who had risen to stardom in the science of understanding people's minds, it was a hoax of some kind. What they were really saying was that new ideas threatened the tightly-woven paradigm of academic psychology.

It has been interesting to watch many, if not most, of the rules and the practices in the field of psychology, therapy, and counseling, change dramatically over the exact same years that self-talk and the idea of rewiring the brain came into popular awareness.

I understand what the psychology/counseling field has gone through. It is a field that grew up on the assumptions of its early leaders, but there was no way to disprove those early assumptions without engaging in endless batteries of tests, most of which had to be supported by financial grants, and not all of which were accurate in their analysis.

Even at the time this evolution was beginning, I believed that some of the then-popular psychological methods were not only wrong, but also potentially dangerous to the client.

As one psychologist friend of mine told me, "I've been working with a client for over a year, and she's not getting any better. Every week, for an hour, we have gone over the problem, and she has gone over the abuses she went through in her past, time after time in our sessions, and she's not getting better."

In any situation like that, I found myself feeling sorry for the client. Every week, for an hour, the therapist was literally helping the client rewire the same abuses over and over again into the client's brain. Instead of creating a new mental picture of the positive opportunities of the future, the therapist was re-recording the negative events of the past, and making the negative programs stronger in the client's brain. And they had been doing that for months! No wonder the therapy sessions weren't working.

Eventually, counseling styles began to change. A new, more scientifically aware generation of counseling modalities began to move in with the new technologies of the twenty-first century.

What happened was that advanced brain-scanning technology began to make it possible for researchers to actually watch the brain form new neural pathways based on the individual's perceptions. They were able to prove in the laboratory that the brain continues to grow new neural connections and change, even through adulthood—they learned that the brain has the ability to rewire itself (*neuroplasticity*) throughout an individual's entire lifetime. (This explained why I had observed even older people make major changes in attitudes they had held for a lifetime. Their

102

brains were still able to rewire themselves in new ways no matter how old they were.)

But even before the new research became broadly available, I had not waited for the world of personal growth or the methods of behavioral therapy to catch up. The general public was not yet aware of the new discoveries in the field of neuroscience when, in 1979, I decided it was time to present the concept of self-talk to the world, and I began the task of writing positive self-talk scripts for the first comprehensive library of recorded self-talk programs.

(The goal was to write and record self-talk scripts for every subject a person wanted to work on—or every attitude a person wanted to change.)

The only way I could undertake this task while I was still working full-time as a consultant, was to change the time I got up each morning—so I would have the massive amount of extra time it would take to write the self-talk scripts.

So I set my alarm for the, to me, impossible hour of *four a.m.*— and every morning for months I got up at four in the morning, forced myself awake (I don't drink coffee), cleared my mind, and wrote self-talk scripts. (I put my alarm clock under my pillow when I went to bed each night so that when the alarm went off, it wouldn't wake my wife when I got up in the dark.)

Then, after going into my study and writing self-talk scripts from four a.m. to six-thirty each morning, I got ready and went to work all day at my consulting job. On Saturdays and Sundays, I didn't have to go to my job, but I still got up and wrote self-talk at four o'clock every morning.

After even a few days of writing self-talk every morning, the extreme fatigue of doing this began to set in. The process became a grueling ordeal, as every bone in my body began to ache. I was doing this because I had a dream to change the world, but the battle I faced every morning came from lack of sleep and the limitations of my own physical body.

Getting up at four in the morning *every* morning, when I did not have to, would have been unusual enough by itself, but what made the situation even more challenging was that I was putting forth an extreme effort to write self-talk that would rewire people's brains—even though it was a concept that, at that time, almost no one had ever heard of, and may not accept, and I was about to dedicate my *life* to taking this unknown concept to the world.

(On behalf of all the positive dreamers who are told again and again that their ideas will never come to pass, let me say this: *Keep the dream. Stay with it. Never quit.* That's what makes dreams happen.)

The self-talk scripts I wrote during that time covered a lot of subjects, dozens of them, including everything from health and fitness, to finances, career, relationships, and self-esteem, among others. And finally, in 1981, that library of self-talk, which I titled *Winning from Within*, the first self-talk audio programs ever offered to the public, was published by the largest self-improvement audio company in the United States.

Because of my earlier experience with language learning, and my more recent experience with listening to self-talk, I knew that the concept worked, but after the audio programs were published and went into public use, and many more people started listening to self-talk cassettes, the vote was in. People responded overwhelmingly positively to listening to self-talk, and attitudes and lives began to change.

Within eighteen months of the time the new self-talk programs were first published, I was asked to appear in a television infomercial on self-talk, and the library of self-talk programs I had written and produced could be purchased by the show's viewers. For the show, the television producers taped an hour-long seminar that I presented to a live studio audience.

The program, entitled *"60 Minutes to Success"* started airing on national cable TV networks, and soon the concept of self-talk was

104

being beamed into living rooms all over North America. I was reaching thousands of viewers with the concept of self-talk, and I was beginning to bring my goal of helping others to life.

The following year, in 1985, I founded the Self-Talk Institute. With that organization, I would be able to reach more people with the message of self-talk, conduct more self-talk training seminars, and continue to do more research on the subject.

It was exactly then that there was a shift in the force.

With my picture of how I could actually contribute to helping change the world finally starting to take form, in the final months of 1985 I left all semblance of a normal life—and went off to an island to write the book *What to Say When You Talk to Your Self.*

I wanted to put everything I had learned into a book that everyone could read. (The story of how that book got written is related in another chapter.)

For the development of self-talk itself—from the first questions I asked, to the first idea of rewiring the brain like learning a new language, to new scientific research, to writing self-talk audio programs, to television shows, to writing books—once the idea of self-talk got going, it was a train that never stopped.

Eventually, technology—and the Internet—made it possible to literally bring self-talk to the world. The self-talk audio programs that I had first written, and had produced on cassettes and then audio CDs, were replaced by new digital self-talk audio sessions that are now streamed to individual smart phones and tablets to self-talk listeners all over the world. (You can listen to self-talk sessions at www.selftalkplus.com.)

I'm *very* thankful that, as all of this began, I had identified my life track of *What? How? When?* because in the years of giving birth to self-talk, if I had not had a clear set of goals, I could have so easily gotten off track.

Now, touching only briefly on the highlights of those years makes it sound like everything always fell into place, everything was blissful, and fortune smiled like sunlight every day. But in the real life of creating self-talk, it did not work that way—not everything fell into place without effort, and fortune only smiled and showered the work with sunlight when I, and often many others, worked eighteen-hour days without stopping.

I don't know today, many years later, how many millions of people have benefited in some way from self-talk—either by changing their self-talk, or because someone around them in their life changed theirs. When I see that happening now, I'm glad I stayed with it. The reason I did was that I wanted to help make the world a better place, and introducing self-talk to the world was a way for me to do that.

I believe it all happened because I was lucky enough to be able to connect the dots. The first was that, because of my experience as a language translator, I made the connection that by changing our self-talk we are teaching the brain a new language—in this case the language of success and of positive, healthy new attitudes.

The second connection I made was my recognition that people genuinely want to live up to their best, as they were created to do, but they often cannot see a true picture of themselves because it has been programmed out of them. And I saw that the right self-talk is redemptive and can give the true success that is their birthright back to them—it gives their lives back to them.

The third connection that helped self-talk come to life was my recognition that for great ideas to grow, they cannot sit still, waiting to happen; they must be given the breath and the energy of life. They have to be presented, and taught, and explained, without stopping, so that people become aware of them and benefit from them, and I chose to devote my life to doing that.

The story of self-talk is about a wonderful kind of redemption for each of us—wiring the brain to be healthy, happy, and successful. It's about letting *everyone* know that the brain is designed to do that. It's about letting people know that they can rewire their brains in the positive. And with that, they can change their lives for the better.

That is my message. That's how *self-talk,* as we know it today, got started.

What I learned:

My greatest lesson in my work with self-talk has been the value of having a significant and undeniable message—one that is foundational to changing lives—and making the choice to present that message to the world, and then making the greater choice to see it through.

When I first began studying the workings of the brain and showed that it could be physically rewired and changed with the right kind of self-talk, only people close to me recognized that I was completely serious in my goal to help people throughout the world learn to change their self-talk—and with that, their lives.

The enormity of the task has been a humbling experience, and it may take another lifetime or two to complete my goal. But in all this time, I have not found a more effective tool for improving lives, and I have never found a more worthwhile goal than telling the world about self-talk. So I am happy with the choice I made then, and the choice I continue to make today. It was the right thing to do.

Chapter Sixteen
Inspiration

It would be impossible to express the importance of the role that self-talk has played in the story of my life, without sharing a story or two of what happens in other people's lives when their destiny brings them into an unexpected conjunction with self-talk.

When my own road gets long, or my energy is low, remembering these stories and so many others like them, gives me the inspiration to stay with it, to keep going, and keep spreading the word.

As one unforgettable example, I had been appearing on television infomercials for several months, presenting a seminar on self-talk on cable networks throughout the U.S., when I received a letter from a man I will call Michael.

Michael wrote to tell me that one night, during an unbelievably dark time in his life, he found himself sitting alone, at home, with nothing left in his spiritual reserves. His life was on "empty," and he had run out of the will to go on. In the past months, Michael had failed in everything he had touched; he had lost his wife and children, then he had lost his job, and then he had lost the last of the faith he once had in himself. Now, with everything that was important to him gone from his life, he could see no way to go on. He no longer wanted to live.

On this particular night, feeling he was at the end of his options, Michael was sitting on the sofa in his living room, holding a gun in his hands, deciding to end it all. He had just decided to get up to go find the bullets to load the gun, when he heard something on the television that was playing in the background.

Still holding his gun in his hand, just as he was getting up, what Michael overheard from the television was someone talking about getting past problems—it was from the self-talk seminar I had appeared on that was being broadcast on television. By coincidence, at that moment, I was on camera saying that it doesn't make any difference how tough things are, what mental programs we have, or how negative they are; we can change our programs, and doing that can change our lives.

When he heard that, Michael sat back down, laid the gun down next to him on the sofa, and watched the rest of the seminar. Whatever he heard in those next few minutes caused him to make the decision to put off ending his life until he had a chance to go back and watch the show from the beginning the next time it came on—so he would be able to hear what he had missed the first time around.

When Michael wrote to me, it was six months later. Shortly after the fateful night he had almost killed himself, he had watched the television show a second time in its entirety. Because of that, he had decided to learn more about self-talk—which led to him practicing it daily—and it had worked. The changes in Michael's life didn't all happen overnight, and it took a lot of work on his part, but he had gotten his wife and children back, he had gotten his job back, and he said he was writing to thank me for giving him his life back.

I felt very moved by his letter, but I knew that I wasn't the one who had given him his life back; Michael did that. But I admit I was very thankful Michael's television set had been tuned to that particular channel that night.

And ever after, any time I started to think how hard it was to do my job of getting the self-talk message out to people through talks, or media tours, or spending grueling hours taping television shows that I wouldn't know if people were watching, I would think of Michael, someone whom I had never met and did not

109

know, and what a few right words at one of the most important moments in his life had meant to him.

Another of the early stories of the effect self-talk was having on people came from a school teacher and one of her students.

When I'm speaking to an audience, I often tell them that if there are any teachers in attendance, I will send to them, as a personal gift from me, self-talk audio programs that they can play in their classrooms. When I first began doing this, self-talk was recorded on audio cassettes, so at that time, I would send the teachers a special set of self-talk cassette programs I had recorded for kids.

As a result of sending self-talk programs to teachers, I would hear back from them, and they would tell me about the success they were having by playing self-talk sessions to their students. Among these, one stood out so strongly that I have never forgotten it.

In this case, I received a letter from a teacher, but along with it, I also received a letter from one of her students.

The teacher told me how she had played the self-talk cassettes I had sent to her, in her class each day. She wrote that she had played them for six weeks by placing a cassette player on an empty desk next to the classroom door at the far front corner of the room, playing the self-talk for about fifteen minutes each day, during a "free time" study period.

One of her problem students, named Billy, was a particularly difficult student. He had a troubled home life; he had no dad that he knew, and his anger at life often got him into trouble. He had lived a tough life, and his brain had been wired for failure.

During the daily study period, the students were permitted to sit wherever they wanted to sit in the classroom. On the day the teacher placed the cassette player on the desk at the far right front of the room, and began playing the positive self-talk sessions, Billy immediately got up and moved as far away from the positive self-talk as he could get—he moved to the far back, rear desk in the *opposite* corner of the room.

The first day the self-talk session was being played, with all of its positive messages, Billy spent the entire time angrily carving pictures into the cover of his notebook with a pocket knife. He was openly refusing to listen to the uplifting self-talk phrases that were coming from the cassette player; they were completely the opposite of what he had been programmed to believe about himself.

In her letter to me, the teacher wrote that when she watched Billy, and saw what he was doing, she decided to neither say, nor do, anything. She just let the self-talk play as I had recommended, out loud, in the background, during the study period.

Each following day, the teacher did the same thing, playing a session of the special program of self-talk for kids at the beginning of the study period, and while she observed the students' various reactions to the self-talk messages, she didn't criticize or question any behavior; she just watched.

And then the teacher started to notice something important. Billy, the troubled boy who started the first day by almost violently fighting against the positive self-talk messages he was hearing, started doing something unusual. After the first few days of hearing the self-talk, he had stopped carving angry pictures into his notebook cover—and then he did something surprising. Billy began to sit in a different desk, one that was no longer in the far opposite corner of the room from the cassette player—he moved to a desk that was a little closer to the cassette player that was playing positive self-talk.

During the six weeks that the teacher played the self-talk each day, she watched as Billy continued to change his seat, and move closer and closer to the desk at the far front corner of the room, the desk with the cassette player that was playing the self-talk.

The teacher wrote that on the final day of the six weeks that she played the self-talk sessions, she watched as Billy came into the room, and sat down in the cassette desk—*the desk with the cassette player on it.*

That alone, would have been a success for the teacher and her decision to keep playing the self-talk. But it was what she saw that day that caused her to write to me. It was something both unexpected and wonderful: When the self-talk was playing, she watched as Billy silently mouthed each word of the self-talk message to himself—having memorized it—repeating it perfectly along with the recording—phrases like: *"I'm on top, in tune, in touch, and going for it!"*

Included with the teacher's letter, there was also a letter addressed to me from Billy. I'll paraphrase it here:

"Dear Dr. Helmstetter. Thank you for self-talk. Thank you for sending it to our teacher so she could play it in our school. Because of self-talk I'm doing better in school. I'm getting better grades now. I don't fight as much with my brother. I can hit the basket from center court. I stopped doing drugs, and I dropped out of the gang. And I'm no longer afraid of the dark."

(Signed) "Billy"

"Age - 16 years old."

It would be wonderful to meet Billy now. I can only imagine the changes that sixteen-year-old kid made in his life, because one of his teachers took the time to play self-talk in her classroom.

And I can also imagine what might have happened if Billy had never had the chance to hear the positive truth about what a quality person he really was, and who he was really born to be.

One of the stories that came to me was from a very serious, practical woman who told me about a most unusual self-talk experience. It's one of those special stories that, while it actually happened, make us think about a higher, helping hand in our lives.

Here is her story:

"My husband and I were sound asleep in our upstairs bedroom when, in the middle of the night, about two in the morning, all of a sudden I was jolted awake by a loud voice repeating self-talk phrases about "taking action now." The voice was coming from the stereo downstairs in the living room, at very high volume. One of the self-talk CDs we had been listening to had somehow turned itself on, and was blaring self-talk phrases very loudly.

"I immediately shook my husband, who hadn't woken up, to tell him I thought someone had broken into our house, and had accidentally turned the stereo on while they were trying to steal it.

"But when I shook my husband, he didn't stir. I shook him again, harder, telling him to wake up, but he didn't move. When I shook him even harder, he didn't respond at all, and I then realized with shock that my husband, who is diabetic, was in a diabetic coma! I immediately went to work to revive him, and then to stabilize him, while all the while the self-talk CD kept playing downstairs on the stereo, and talking about "taking action now."

"It took a while, but when my husband finally came back to life, and was able to be awake and aware, we went downstairs together, slowly, cautiously, turning all the lights on. We found that the house was locked up tight, and that no one had broken in. We turned off the self-talk CD that had been playing on the stereo, and eventually calmed down and went back to bed.

"The next day we had the stereo completely checked out, and discovered that there was no way it could have started playing all by itself.

"But it did. If it weren't for the self-talk suddenly turning itself on and playing loudly in the middle of the night, talking about *taking action now*, I would not have woken up, I would not have found my husband in a coma, I would not have revived him, and he might not be alive today."

I know there should be some practical, earthly reason that the stereo came on by itself, although they never found one. But it's good to know that stereos can turn on in the middle of the night at exactly the right time, just when someone needs help most.

In some ways, it has been equally inspiring to me to watch what has transpired in the fields of "motivation" and "personal growth." As authors, speakers, and trainers learned about self-talk, they began to share it with their readers and audiences—and they began to help get the word out. Over a period of years, the personal growth industry began to add the brain science of self-talk to its core message of setting goals, self-belief, and winning attitudes; self-talk was a key element in the foundation of the principals they were teaching.

The result of this broad acceptance of the message of self-talk was that on any given day the top names in the personal growth field were talking about self-talk from stage or writing about it in their books. I was humbled by that. And I was very thankful that I was not alone.

What I learned:

Having so many people tell me their stories of what happened when self-talk entered their lives, gave me the assurance that I was on the right track with my life's goal—and I could move forward with confidence, and keep going. It's like getting the report card that motivates you to keep striving to do your best. And so many times it was the people in my audience, or the ones I would hear from by mail or email, whose positive votes kept me going.

(What I learned from the story of the man in the diabetic coma, when the stereo came on for no reason at all, reaffirmed to me one more time that miracles really do happen.)

And what I learned when the ideas I had been presenting started to be supported and applied by other authors and speakers, was that self-talk is an idea whose time has come.

Chapter Seventeen
Finding the Key

When I graduated from high school, because of my early goal to become a minister, and because of a lack of money at home, there had never been any consideration given to my doing anything other than entering a seminary and going into the ministry. In doing that, my family would receive financial help from the church to send me to school, so I could afford to go.

But when I decided that my calling was for a different path, and I decided not to enter the ministry, I found myself with the same questions and options that a lot of young men face after leaving school.

At the time, just fifteen years after the end of World War II, going into the military service was a popular option. I also thought that seeing the world and learning something about it wasn't a bad idea. So I visited a Navy recruiting office, took a bunch of tests, was promised I would be sent to school, and raised my hand. Less than a month later, still seventeen years old, I was in the United States Navy.

I did well in the Navy. I don't think it was because I was by nature cut out for military service—I probably wasn't—but what I *was* good at was understanding "the system," working hard, and staying out of trouble. The military also spent a lot of time testing recruits during their first months in the service, and my test results told some analyst somewhere that I was a candidate for language training.

After waiting for the government security-checkers to do their background investigations, they concluded that I was not a security risk, and I was available for a job that required a high level security clearance. With that taken care of, the Navy loaned me to the Army, and sent me to the U.S. Army Language School, (later the Defense Language Institute), in Monterey, California.

At the time, I had no idea how important the next few months would be to my future work. While studying the Spanish language in preparation for becoming a Spanish/English interpreter, I learned how the brain can become programmed with a completely new language, just by being immersed in that language day after day.

On the very first day of classes, when the other students and I walked into the classroom, the instructor of that class, who was from Chile, said "Hola," ("Hello," in Spanish). And from that moment on, for the next six months, not a single English word was spoken by him or any other of our instructors—nor were we as students, at any time, allowed to speak a word of English.

Even on field trips, only Spanish was spoken, both by the instructors and by the students. One day, while on a field trip to the Mission San Juan Bautista, I asked the instructor, who was from Spain, why he never, ever spoke to us in English. His reply to me, in perfect Castilian Spanish was, "Yo no hablo Inglés." He did not speak the English language.

My highest accolade while I was studying Spanish at the Army Language School was that one month, out of two or three thousand students—almost all of them Army soldiers—I received the *"Soldier* of the Month" award. I was proud of it, but I found it was an uncomfortable award to receive, as someone who was in the Navy, and who was clearly not a "soldier." I'm not sure I had a lot of Army friends for a while after that.

It was not long after graduation that I found myself on a military transport plane headed for Cuba. The U.S. Naval facility at Guantanamo Bay had a team of Spanish/English translators in place, who, while working in a high security position, were clearly watching what was going on at the time between Cuba's Russian-leaning leader, Fidel Castro, and the safety of the U.S. homeland.

The only truly, personally dangerous time I experienced while I was in Cuba, was when, on a day off, I went exploring in a small fishing skiff with two of my teammates who were also language interpreters, and we ended up in territory we didn't recognize.

We were rowing along the underbrush that overhung a river we were navigating, when we heard people talking—and we were about to shout out to them when we realized they weren't speaking Spanish or English—they were speaking *Russian!* We peered through the thick undergrowth and saw, not thirty feet from us, a group of about ten Russian soldiers, and we realized that by mistake, we had rowed our small skiff out of U.S. territory and into the forbidden zone.

With international tensions as tightly-wound as they were at the time, being Spanish/English interpreters for the U.S. Government, and being caught or captured by Russian soldiers would be a very bad thing. (The Cuban and Russian governments called our work "spying.")

The Russian soldiers were all armed with automatic rifles, and the three of us in the skiff were unarmed; none of us had so much as a pocket knife with us, and the only thing we could do was attempt to steal away as silently as we could. As we moved slowly away, we were rowing silently, trying not to breathe, and praying hard, all at the same time.

When we finally got back into the safe, deep U.S. territorial waters of the bay, closer to the U.S. Naval base, the water was choppy, with strong waves, and it was difficult to make any headway, but at least we felt we were out of danger. That is, until we noticed a giant Navy seaplane bearing down on us, getting lower and closing fast, and flying just a few feet above the waves.

Then the seaplane's huge pontoon belly hit the water, sending up a blanket of spray as it came straight for us, and we all threw ourselves to the bottom of the boat as the plane lifted up, its engines roaring, and passed only a few feet above us, the water pouring off its pontoon fuselage, drenching us. The airplane's pilots hadn't even seen us!

We were badly shaken up, but we were greatly relieved to have not gotten hit by the plane, and were all breathing a heavy sigh of relief, when we saw the seaplane circle and head back toward us again. It was then that we realized we were directly in the middle of the Navy sea plane practice zone where that plane, and two others like it, were doing touch-and-goes, hitting the water and then lifting, circling around and coming back for the next run. I have never seen three guys in a skiff row so fast. We made it out of danger, and we made it back to our base, and I never again went out in a skiff on a day off.

As the days went by, I was all too aware that there was an actual danger threatening all of us. It was on the island of Cuba, working as an interpreter, sixteen feet underground in the reinforced concrete and steel of the Admiral's command bunker, that I listened, barely breathing, to President John F. Kennedy's speech to the world, telling everyone what my teammates and I already knew—that we had discovered Soviet nuclear missiles en route to Cuba, and that missile launch sites that had been constructed there were close to completion. What would be called "The Cuban Missile Crisis" had begun.

When I had originally left the U.S. for Cuba, my wife was pregnant, and my infant son Anthony came into the world while I was away. That, in itself, was tough enough, but it was especially difficult being in an underground bunker in Cuba, translating minute-by-minute messages from people on the ground, to government officials who were in the command bunker deciding the future of the world. I had never seen my little son, and he and my wife were very far away. And in that bunker in Cuba, I knew how very fragile their future, and the future of the world, really was. We actually were within a breath of nuclear war.

At the time, I often wondered what all of this was for—why I was diverging so far off my ordained course in life—the one in which I wanted to change the world. I had already known that there would be a reason and a purpose in my life, but if I got out of Cuba alive, I couldn't see how being there, at the center of a global conflict, could play any meaningful role in my future path.

Of course, it was easy for me to see that I was learning about duty, and service to others, on the broadest scale, and also about personal responsibility. (I often wondered, what if I had translated one of those critical messages incorrectly, and it had changed the outcome of the crisis?)

But I was also learning another lesson. Much later I would recognize that learning a language and becoming a good interpreter held one of the most vital clues to the programming of the human mind—something I would need to know for my life's work. And to make sure I would remember the language lesson, I had been placed at the epicenter of one of the most unforgettable moments of an entire century.

What I learned:

What I discovered about learning a new language set up the key I would need later, to help people change their mental language from one of self-doubt to one of self-belief. In the brain, learning a new self-dialogue is the same as learning a new language.

Although I was not aware of it at the time, it is clear to me now that I went through language training to ingrain in me, soundly, the awareness that learning a language, and learning to interpret our thoughts—and change them—are at the core of changing our programming. That knowledge was essential to what I would one day need to know.

(As a footnote to my experiences in Cuba, I could not have known at the time that one day, many years later, my books would be published in the Russian language, and could today be being read by the same people who were once the Russian soldiers we almost ran into in Cuba—who at the time, we saw as enemies. Nor could I have known that today, among the people I have taught to become professional Self-Talk Trainers, there are people from countries with which we were once at war.)

Chapter Eighteen
Writing

One of the first things I was sure of in my life was that I was going to write. When I was seven years old, my sister Holly, who was eight, and I, wrote our first published work.

We had, together, written a poem, which we thought was good enough to be published in a magazine. But we didn't know how to get it published, so we printed it out in hand lettering on a sheet of notebook paper and took it to the local post office in our small town and asked to talk to someone who could help us.

A kind, older man, the postmaster, came out from behind the service window to talk to us, and we explained to him that we wanted to get our poem published in a magazine. He must have liked our determination, because he took our poem, along with a letter we had written about the poem, and carefully put the two pieces of paper in an envelope. He addressed the envelope to Augsburg Publishing, which was the publishing company for his church. He then sealed the envelope, put a stamp on it, and put it in that day's outgoing mail.

A few weeks later, Holly and I received a letter saying our poem had been selected for publication, and sometime after that, we received a copy of the magazine with our poem in it. I'm sure I must have immediately (and mistakenly) thought how *easy* it is to write something and get it published.

But it wasn't always smooth sailing. Far from it. I'll share an example with you, of an event in my life that could have ended my writing career before it began.

One of the first challenges I faced was when I was still in high school, and I had an early dream of writing a book. In fact, I had done more than think about it; I had started on a manuscript—the beginnings of an actual book in its unedited form.

As a student, I was unsure about showing my book to anyone, but I overcame my hesitation, and on a Friday, at the end of the last class of the day, I decided to ask my English teacher if she would read my manuscript.

I stayed after class after all of the other students had left, and with some trepidation, I took my book manuscript up to my teacher, Mrs. Thompson, and asked her if she would read it.

She smiled at me, I think somewhat dismissively, and said she would look at it over the weekend.

What followed was probably the longest weekend of my life. I assumed my teacher knew everything there was to know about books and grammar and words, everything there was to know about writing. All I would have to do was to be able to wait through the weekend. On Monday, I would have the first review of my book, and I was certain it would be a good review. That would give me the motivation I needed to finish the book and maybe actually get it published. I wanted to hear from someone else, who I respected, that I could do it.

Finally, Monday arrived. Mrs. Thompson's class was the last class of the day, so it was hard to be patient and wait. Eventually, it was time. I walked into Mrs. Thompson's class, sat down in my desk, and waited for the class to end—so I could hear from Mrs. Thompson, one-on-one, that I had a book that was well-written, full of merit, and would be sure to become a best-seller. What happened next could have sent my life in one of two very different directions.

At the end of the class period, just before excusing the rest of the class for the day, Mrs. Thompson called my name, and asked me to remain after class. After the classroom had emptied out, and

I was the only student remaining, I walked up to the front row of student desks and sat in the center one, right in front of the teacher's desk.

I have never forgotten what happened next.

While I sat in a lowly student desk, Mrs. Thompson sat on the front corner of her teacher's desk, directly in front of me, and above me. She held my sacred manuscript in her hands, and I recall vividly how she kind of slammed my manuscript on her knee, as she shook her head and said, *"You will never write a best-selling book."*

And then, so as to further motivate me, she went on to tell me *why* I would never write a best-selling book, let alone write a book of any kind. She told me I didn't have the skill; my grammar wasn't good enough; I didn't have what it takes to see it through; and out of the tens of thousands of books published each year, there are only a few books that make it into the best-seller category—and almost no one has a chance of making it.

I was crushed and humiliated. I accepted my manuscript as Mrs. Thompson handed it back to me, and I remember that when I left the school, I walked home very, very slowly. When I got home, I took my manuscript and put it on the top shelf of the closet in my bedroom, and never took it down again.

It was years later that I finally figured out that Mrs. Thompson had been wrong. Her criticism was actually born out of her own lack of self-belief and deeply-programmed doubts she had about herself—and it had had nothing to do with me in the first place. It was *her* fear, not mine. (I suspect that she had wanted to write a book herself, but was afraid she would fail.) Because of her fear, she had given her negative mental programs to me, and for a time, I had accepted them.

I was fortunate to have eventually figured that out, and in time, I decided that if I wanted to write a book, nothing was going to stop me.

I wrote notebooks full of stories and essays throughout my school years, but my first serious attempts at writing were when I was in high school. On one of those occasions, I was turned down for a writing position on the school paper because I wasn't enrolled in a journalism class. I didn't have any space in my schedule to fit in a journalism class, so I decided to take a different tack.

I wrote an article I thought would be topical and interesting. Then, I signed my article with a pen name, and one day, after everyone had gone home for the day, I slipped the article under the door of the journalism department. And then I waited.

Two weeks later, there was my article, several columns in length, published in its entirety in the school paper. Beneath the article, there was a note asking that the writer of the article come to the journalism department. So that day after class I met with the head of the journalism department and explained that I had written the article. He asked me if I could write any more articles like the one they had published, and I answered him by handing him the next article that I had already written. I got the job.

The school paper continued to publish my articles, and the students liked them. It was because of those articles that when an opening came up for a student reporter to write a weekly commercial column for the city newspaper, I was offered the position. I took the job, and it turned out to be my first paying writing assignment. It didn't pay as much as doing yard work, but it was a lot more fun.

As I grew older, I continued to write, but still not as a vocation. As an adult I wrote another weekly column for a daily newspaper, and later, a regular column for a national travel magazine. But like many people who want to write, I had the dream, but I hadn't gotten *serious* about it. Writing, for me, in any serious way, was still waiting for its purpose.

Then one day I wrote down a goal on a blue-colored 5X8 index card (I used blue cards to write out my most important goals). The goal I wrote that day said:

My Goal is: "To write a best-selling book that will be published around the world, that will help people improve their lives."

It was writing out the goal that changed everything.

Writing the goal in specific words—where I could see it and read it every day—changed entirely how I thought about writing a book, and what I would do to bring my dream to life. Because I read my goal cards every morning, and every night just before I went to sleep, what I was actually doing was wiring those completed goal pictures—of having an actual published book— into the neuron pathways in my brain.

The first evidence of wiring that goal into my brain was my decision to write the book *What to Say When You Talk to Your Self.*

I had already been working at telling the world about my discoveries in how the human brain gets wired to succeed or fail through an individual's own self-talk. I had appeared in several popular television infomercials, and that was helping me reach audiences of late-night television viewers with the story of self-talk. By the time I decided to write a book on the subject, the infomercials were running nightly on cable networks, and self-talk was becoming a topic that was gaining attention. I decided it was time for the book to be written.

I also decided it was time to adopt a creative approach to writing it; I would write the entire book where I would be in my most creative element—by the *water.* At the time, I was living in Scottsdale, Arizona, in the middle of the desert, so the first thing I did for my writing project was to call a rental condo located on Mustang Island, off the coast of Texas. I wanted to rent a condo, right on the water, on the Gulf of Mexico, for the three months of October, November, and December. That was past tourist season and into the fall and winter, so there were plenty of rental units available, and off I went.

As it turned out, I would be one of only two inhabitants of a huge condo building on the water. At least I *think* there was someone else renting there, because sometimes I would see a light on at night on in a window on the far side of the U-shaped condo complex. But I never actually saw or met the other renter the entire time I was there.

I mention this lack of human presence because the extreme isolation of the next three months added profoundly to my writing experience. Being alone for an extended period of time can be a unique experience in itself. But being alone day after day in a large, deserted beachfront condo, as the sky grows dark and overcast and winter sets in, is more like living in a movie set than living in real life.

I had a large cardboard box of notes that I had amassed over many months of research for my book, and I had brought that box with me when I flew to the island to write. But when I arrived at the condo and was unpacking and getting settled in, I took the large box of notes—without opening it—and hoisted it onto the top shelf of one of the condo's bedroom closets. I wanted to start fresh. The box of notes stayed closed the entire time I was there.

The condo I had selected was on the fourth floor, high up so I would have a good view of the water. I set up my computer and printer on a table in one of the main rooms that had a full wall of floor-to-ceiling windows overlooking the beach and the large expanse of the Gulf of Mexico.

With that done, and being all moved in, I was almost ready to write. There was just one more essential thing I planned to do before I started writing, one of the reasons I had chosen this quiet place on the water to write in the first place: I wanted to *walk on the beach and create the future.*

127

And that's what I did. For the first two weeks I was on the island, I didn't write a single word on my book. Every day I just walked the beach and talked to myself about the book I had come there to write.

The chilly, cloud-shadowed autumn mornings would find me, my jacket collar pulled up around my neck to keep warm, walking the beach, talking out loud to the sky and the seagulls, and the sandpipers scurrying along the sand next to the water's edge. The only footprints in the sand, walking up and down the beach each day, were my own.

The reason I walked the beach and talked to myself was because I knew that whatever picture I wired into my mind would influence what would end up being written on every page, in every paragraph, in every sentence I would write.

My self-talk during those beach walks each day was that I was going to write a book that would help people all over the world. I told myself that it would become a "classic" and that it would still be in stores and people would still be reading it twenty years after the time I wrote it.

When I told myself I was going to write a classic book, or a book that would last for twenty years, I was not trying to kid myself or be falsely positive. I knew that if I was setting out to write a book that would last, and if I clearly imprinted that picture in my mind, that single choice would be reflected in everything I wrote. It would change the book. It would make it better.

I should add that at the time I was walking on the beach talking to myself for those two weeks, I had no reason to believe I could even write a book—let alone a book that would be successful—other than the fact that I was *choosing to believe* that I could write it. Day after day, that's what I was wiring into my brain.

At the end of two weeks, after walking up and down the beach talking to myself every day, I went up to my almost empty condo, sat down at the table I had set up for writing, and turned on my computer. Then I put one of the cassette tapes of special music I had brought with me into a cassette player, turned on the music, opened the computer screen to a blank word-processing page, and wrote the opening sentences of the book:

"You are everything that is,
Your thoughts, your life, your dreams come true.
You are everything you choose to be.
You are as unlimited as the endless universe."

Each night, often at two or three in the morning, when I would stop writing for that day, I would pause the music right where I stopped writing. The next day, when I began writing again, I would start the music again at that same place I had paused it the night before, and the music would automatically take my mind right back to where it had been when I had stopped writing. By always using music as my mental writing field, I didn't have to struggle to get back on track the next day; the music took me there.

I had chosen specific music to write to, and had brought cassette tapes of my selections with me to the island. I listened to one type of music for being creative, opening up ideas and expanding my mind. I listened to another type of music for heightening my emotions when I was writing about feelings. As an example, I would listen to warm, rich, emotional music when I wanted the tone of what I was writing at the moment to be heartfelt and personal, just as I was feeling it. Then, later, when I was editing the chapter to get it structured and formed just right, I would play a completely different kind of music—classical baroque music—which is very structured and organized.

The result of listening to specific songs or musical passages as I was writing was that I created a mental soundtrack to the entire book. (Today, over three decades later, when I listen to those same tracks of music, I am immediately taken back to sitting at my computer in the condo on the beach when I was writing to that particular music. Each of those musical selections remains, today, the soundtrack of that book.)

For the next two-and-a-half months, as I continued to write each day, and late into the night, I also continued to take daily walks on the beach—not as much as I had during the first two weeks before I began my writing—but I would walk on the beach some, each day. I almost had the feeling that some of the little sandpipers, scurrying along the dunes as I walked, were getting to know me.

While I was there, I continued to use self-talk each day. I would listen to the pre-recorded cassettes of self-talk when I was getting ready in the condo each morning, and I would often talk out loud, to the waves and the sandpipers, as I walked along the beach.

I do not recall a single time during my writing that I ever questioned what I was doing, or doubted whether my objective of reaching the world with my message would be successful. I knew I was correct about the concept I was writing about, and I knew that all I had to do was to put it into words—clear, plain, simple words.

Looking back on that time, what I had done when I isolated myself on an island, I realized, was to leave my safe, ordinary, day-to-day life behind me. I had forced myself to write in an environment of solitude, a place that was without daily human interaction or support. I had walked, day after day, on a beach that was made up of possibilities instead of sand. And day after day, each day I wrote, I demanded of myself that I write a book that would reach my goal.

My idea of writing a book in this way worked. My first goal of eventually seeing that book still being published and still on the shelves of bookstores twenty years later, came true, and then it kept going beyond that.

After the book was published, it never left the self-help best-seller lists. As I write this now, thirty-some years later, *What to Say When You Talk to Your Self* has been published in more than seventy countries around the world, and the list of countries grows every year.

I don't mention any of this to make something special of my writing a book, or to pat myself on the back for writing it. I mention it because it was all about the *goal* of writing it, and knowing that it was a part of my goal to help people improve their lives; it was a book that had found its purpose.

After *What to Say When You Talk to Your Self* was published, I continued writing and I found other places where I also like to write.

On my later books, I've done some of my writing in the mountains of Arizona, and some of that time, I wrote while I was on horseback. At that time, I was using a small cassette recorder, the kind used for dictation. I found that I could write while I was on a trail horse, ambling slowly on mountain trails. I found, however, that writing by dictation uses different parts of the brain than writing by typing out your thoughts on a keyboard. The chapters I dictated into a voice recorder were softer, more conversational, while the chapters I typed on a keyboard have always been more structured and organized.

Other locations that have been good writing places have been on the beach in Virginia Beach, Virginia, on Mobile Bay on the coast of Alabama, and on Pensacola Beach, Florida. By "on the beach" I don't mean to say I sit in a beach chair and soak up the sun while I write. But in each case I find a room to write in where I'm able to see water, as much of it as possible, horizon to horizon. There's a reason for this.

131

When I'm on a coastal shore and I stand at the water's edge and look out over the water, I can imagine that I'm seeing the same scene that someone a thousand years before me, standing on the exact same spot, also saw. If I can't see any human-made structures in my peripheral vision to either side of me, my view of the world at that moment is *exactly* what some other person saw, eons of time before I was born, and in my mind I can bridge the time between the two of us.

Standing on that shore creates a strong sense of perspective for me, a broader picture of life, and my almost-less-than-visible place in it. It moves me from being a random participant to being an observer; and it takes me beyond the grand illusion of everyday life and opens a window to a picture that is much bigger than all of us—much bigger than we can possibly imagine. When I write on the water, I may not be right at the water's edge, but I get as close to the water, to that view, and to that perspective—that larger, broader picture of life—as I can.

Some time ago, I was going through an old file box filled with odds and ends of things, papers and other mementos that I had tucked away over the years. In the middle of this collection of keepsakes I came across an old, worn, 5X8 blue index card. On the card, printed out by hand, were the words: *My Goal is: "To write a best-selling book that will be published around the world, that will help people improve their lives."*

It was the goal card that took the dream I had as a boy—when I wanted to do something to change the world—and it created the action step that would help translate the dream into action. Without writing those words on that card, I'm not sure what might have happened to that dream.

What I learned:

I know that you can learn important things in creative writing classes in school, but at some point you have to sit down and write, and it will have to come from you.

Writing is one of those beautiful brain-enhancing activities, and a healthy exercise I would recommend to anyone. The brain loves a challenge that cannot be quite met. And that's what writing is—a perfect challenge. No matter how hard you work at it, or for how long, tomorrow you will always face another empty page, waiting for you to fill it up. As long as I am here, I hope to always have another empty page in front of me.

My creative writing class was an island, a seashore, and some sandpipers. I learned that what I needed to do most was to have a clear goal in mind, and then simply to *write*. I needed to work hard at it, day after day, shaping my ideas and my thoughts into word pictures that would hopefully make sense. Most of all, I needed to make sure the word pictures I was creating would come to *life* and connect with the readers I was imagining, a half a world away, and decades later, no matter who that reader might be.

It was during the time I spent on that island, that I came face to face with the destiny I had felt so compelled to follow. This was the moment that the dream of the boy in the wheat field truly began to come to life.

Chapter Nineteen
On Stage

The first time I spoke publicly, giving a speech I had memorized, was when I entered a regional speaking contest as a ninth-grader in school.

For the contest, I wrote a speech entitled *Are We Free?* It was about being controlled by our own biases and prejudices. (It was an anti-prejudice speech.) My message was that we only *think* we're free, but we're really governed by our programmed beliefs, whatever they are—and what we grow up learning, determines what we think and who we become. I didn't know it at the time, but that first school speech I wrote was about *"mental programming,"*—though I didn't, yet, know the term. It was the precise subject I would focus on years later when I began formulating my thoughts on positive self-talk.

I won the speech contest, for which I was grateful, and came in first at my level of competition, and I received a beautiful award pin that I was very proud of. Then, a few days later, I was notified that due to a clerical error, according to the speech contest rules, I was too young, by two weeks, to have entered the contest, and the honor was withdrawn. (They didn't ask for my award pin back, however, and my mother kept it on her dresser in her small metal box of keepsakes for the rest of her life.)

When it comes to public speaking, I've been very fortunate. It's true that having to speak in front of an audience is one of the worst fears that many people have. But I was fortunate. From the time I first spoke in that ninth grade contest, and after, I did not experience a single time when I had that fear. I don't think it was that I was tough, or strong, or impassioned or anything like that. I just didn't fear the audience.

The smallest public audience I've talked to was twelve people. The largest audience I've talked to was over thirty-six thousand people. I wasn't afraid to talk to either of those audiences. In each case, and everything in between, I believe the real reason I didn't fear those audiences was because I saw them not as an "audience," but as individuals, and I was there to talk to them about something that could help them in their lives.

So I didn't think about public speaking as something to fear; I thought of it as a chance to talk to people, to connect with them, and share something with them. (I had something I really wanted to say.)

I do not know how many talks I've given, or seminars I've presented. I know that I've spoken in front of a live audience thousands of times, and I'm thankful for every one of those opportunities I've had to speak. I had a goal to speak, to reach people with the message of self-talk, and the life I chose gave me the opportunity to do that.

But while each of those speaking events was important to me, I never thought that public speaking or conducting seminars would be anything more than a footnote to the story of my life.

If life's purpose was pictured as a ladder, speaking to audiences was just one of the rungs on that ladder. To me, public speaking was no different than any other part of the work I was doing. (But there were times when it seemed like speaking took up *all* the rungs on the ladder.)

As I talked about in an earlier chapter, I used to imagine that the sound of the wind in the wheat was applause when I was a kid, practicing speaking in wheat fields. But to my surprise, when I actually began to speak in front of live audiences, I found that I almost never heard the audience's applause.

135

It wasn't that I was hearing impaired, or that the people weren't applauding at the end of my talks; something in my brain simply tuned out the applause.

That happened so frequently that if you were to ask me a minute after I left the stage if the audience had applauded politely, or if they had applauded enthusiastically, or if I had gotten a wild standing ovation, I would have absolutely no idea what the audience had done. It isn't some form of false modesty; I love my audiences, and I hope I do a fantastic job of reaching them every time I speak. I just don't hear applause.

My professional opinion on this is that I tune out the applause because to me, it isn't about the applause. It's about the *message*—and not about the *messenger*. That's a conscious choice I made when I started writing about self-talk, and then started speaking about it.

Playing up the *message* and playing down the *messenger* was different from public speakers I knew at the time. I knew a lot of public speakers. In particular, I knew a lot of motivational speakers, and although I respected most of them, as odd as it sounds, I was determined *not* to be one of them. Even though at the time, if you wanted to be a speaker, being a motivational speaker was the popular thing to do, I was determined *not* to follow the trend.

I would, throughout my speaking career, almost never allow myself to be billed or promoted as a motivational speaker. I felt that it was too easy to step over the line from presenting a message to entertaining an audience—and I wanted to be there because of the message. Of course, it's important to be interesting, and to hold the audience's attention, but I had seen many good speakers I really liked, step over that line and become entertainers. Their message was important, but it got missed entirely.

When someone would tell me what a great speaker someone was, I would ask, "What did he *say?*" or "What did she *say?*" In my own speaking, I wanted to be the kind of speaker whose message was so clear and so helpful that everyone in my audience could tell you what my message was—years after they had attended my talk.

(This does not apply, of course, to speakers whose actual job it is to entertain the audience or to pep them up and get them wildly excited to be there. I've known speakers who do this brilliantly, and I admire their skill.)

Along with not wanting to be seen as an entertainer, I also admit that I had an early suspicion of another popular kind of speaker—the "guru"—and I knew I didn't want to be one.

By "guru" I mean the standard American audience *speaker–author–motivator–trainer* guru. When I was speaking at an event along with other speakers, I often preceded or followed "gurus" on stage. This gave me the opportunity to watch and listen to them, usually from the backstage area.

Their performances were often astonishing to me. I know it can be a big job to hold an audience and imbue them with the kind of "stand up and cheer" enthusiasm you would typically see in a religious revival meeting. But I just didn't want my audience to see me as someone they had to react to like that. It wasn't about the messenger; it was about the *message*.

As a practicing gracious and caring person, I never publicly criticized a single one of those speakers to anyone, nor would I, but when they were speaking, I would often personally cringe for them. I could feel it in my stomach.

I would be thinking, *Why is he doing that? No one in the audience is believing him. No one is going to remember what he said.* Is he entertaining? *Yes.* Is he believable? *No.* Will you remember him? *Maybe.* Will you remember what he said? *Probably not.*

So each time I spoke to an audience, I made the conscious decision that I would always make it about the message and just be myself. For the rest of my life, any time I spoke, that was going to be my rule. I would be me—but I was going to be me *with a message*.

If I was going to stick to my rule, I knew I would have to learn how to hold my audiences in other ways, without the showmanship I so determinedly wanted to avoid. So I had to find a solution. And it is this solution that I share with others who are learning to speak professionally.

My solution was to make the decision to a) always genuinely *care* about the people I'm talking to—never fake it; and b) always be myself.

That decision made years of speaking something that I would always look forward to, and I've always enjoyed it immensely. If someone were to ask me, "If you could be doing anything in the world right now, what would it be?" one of my answers would be, "Standing in front of a few hundred, or a few thousand people, for an hour or two talking to them." To me, that's a perfect Saturday afternoon.

It's clear to me that one of the reasons I've enjoyed public speaking so much is that I followed my own rules. I did nothing to try to do it like other people were doing it. I've never tried to play follow-the-leader. Just because everyone else is doing it one way, does not mean that I will do it the same way.

One example of this is the idea of speakers handing out critique sheets. It's a popular thing for public speakers and seminar presenters to hand out critique sheets that ask their audiences to grade various elements of their performance as a speaker.

They do this hoping to get an accurate appraisal of how well they did, or what they could improve, so they can fine-tune their presentation and do it better next time. Unfortunately, with most audiences, the whole idea of critique sheets goes entirely against both practical rules of behavioral psychology and common sense. If you ask someone to critique your presentation, *they will*— whether they know anything about critiquing or not.

Unless you're giving that presentation to people who are knowledgeable and skilled in professional critiquing, you will almost never get back critiques that will help you. What you *will* get is a stack of critique sheets that will keep you awake at night, causing you to lose faith in yourself and doubt your presentation.

If you really want critical input, ask two or three trusted, professional, knowledgeable friends to give you their input. They'll give you their opinions. And even with that, trust your own instincts. If you're being open with your audience, if you're being your honest self, you will be fine. You'll always know if you're getting through. Just watch your audience, and you'll know.

There is another public stage rule I have often been told, and it's another one that should be ignored. For years people have said that if you don't experience stage fright just before you go on stage, you're not really "in the moment" and you won't do your best.

Wrong. Stage fright is a completely individual thing. If it helps you to feel anxiety and tension before your presentation, use it to help you deliver. If you *don't* feel it, don't worry about it. It could be that you're prepared and confident—you've *got* this one. I don't experience pre-talk anxiety *ever,* and I don't get stage fright. That's my self-talk, and that's my choice.

When I'm going to speak, my two overriding choices—*to always care about the people I'm talking to,* and *to always be myself*—have kept me from playing any kind of role that was not me. Those two choices kept me from ever being tempted to try to be a guru. Those two choices kept me from becoming an on-stage performer, there to entertain an audience instead of delivering a meaningful message. And those two choices are probably what kept me from hearing the applause.

There is an almost spiritual postscript to my experiences in public speaking that I would be remiss if I did not mention in this autobiography. It is one of those unusual things that I could not ignore, something I shared with people close to me, and I would like to share it with you.

I was presenting a seminar on stage in a large auditorium. I remember that it was an audience of five or six hundred attendees. During a break in the seminar, a middle-aged professional-looking man, who had been waiting in line to talk to me, came up to where I was standing in front of the stage and said he wanted to speak to me privately. There were a lot of other seminar attendees gathered around, so I suggested we step off to the side, a few feet away from the others, so he could talk without being overheard.

What he said might have been ignored by some people. But I listened to him, and I was uplifted by what he said.

He looked directly at me and said, "I have never had anything like this happen before. I attend church, but I don't know anything about this kind of thing."

And then he continued, "But I have to tell you what I saw. When you were standing up there on the stage today, the entire time you were talking, I saw two figures, really tall, in white robes, standing, one on each side of you."

When I asked him to tell me more, he answered, "I was watching them the whole time," he said. "They were both there, very tall, kind of glowing, all the time you were talking." He then told me again what a completely unusual experience this had been, repeating that he had never experienced anything like this in his life. But he had seen something that was very real to him.

I didn't make light of his experience. This was one of the most sincere, practical-sounding individuals I could have met. I thanked him sincerely and then walked back to the next person in line. I wanted to talk longer to the man who had seen the spirits or whatever they were, but there were other people waiting.

Before then, I had always enjoyed speaking to audiences. But I felt even better about speaking after that. I actually felt at times, standing on a stage in front of an audience by myself, that maybe I wasn't really by myself.

What I learned:

I have been fortunate to be able to speak for many years, and to reach nearly every audience I wanted to reach. I have done exactly what I dreamed of doing when I was a boy, speaking to the wheat.

But I recognized very early that my purpose in getting in front of an audience would not be just for the sake of speaking; it would be because I had something to say that I felt was important for my audience to hear.

Because of my self-imposed rule of making my goal to speak always be about the message, and never about me, although I had the opportunity to do so, I decided not to list my name with speakers' bureaus or booking agencies, and I never did. My interest was not in speaking for a fee (honorarium); I was only interested in being on stage to present my message. To me, public speaking was a method of delivery, but never the goal itself.

That's not to imply that the way I've looked at speaking would be the right approach for someone else; it's solely about the reason speaking was important in my own life—and why I practiced speaking in the wheat fields in the first place.

Chapter Twenty
The Media

To begin my thoughts on the media, and to get it right, I want to make it clear that "the media"—in this case, being on television and radio shows for things like doing a book tour—is absolutely *nothing* like "the media" for being rich and famous and being a media celebrity. The *only* thing the two have in common is that people see you, in both instances, on television, or they hear you on radio, or they read about you in a magazine. That's it.

When I talk about the hundreds of television and radio shows I've been on, the first thing some people think is about being "famous"—red carpet, paparazzi, glamour and lights. I've never seen it that way. When you're using the media as a communications tool, it may *look* like a form of celebrity, but it isn't—it's working hard, telling people about your idea. When you see the media in that way, you'll see the media as it really is.

With that accurate "hard work" image of the media in mind, you'll understand that it's not about media celebrity when I say that I'm not sure how many hundreds of radio and television shows I've been on. I officially stopped counting when the number of personal appearances reached twelve hundred. I think the actual number of television and radio shows I've been invited to appear on is now past two thousand. (I stopped counting because I didn't think most people would believe that number anyway. They would think it was a number that was made up by my publicist.)

The reason I was called on to be on all of those talk shows and news programs was that my books are perfect for talk show hosts and news people to talk about. I write about things that people are interested in—subjects like self-esteem, raising kids, money, personal achievement, or even why we vote the way we do in elections, and specifically, how our brains get wired and how that brain wiring affects our success in life—so there's always something that a good talk show host can turn into a good interview.

When you're on a media tour for a book, and doing six or eight interviews in a day, and then traveling to the next city and doing the same thing again, day after day for two or three months, it can seem like all of the interviews are alike. But they're not. Some of them stand out and are remembered. I'll give you an example.

I was in Boston, Massachusetts, scheduled to be on a mid-morning television show. For most media tours, in each city the publisher arranges to have a media "host," a person whose job it is to drive you to each of your appointments. Usually the media host picks you up at your hotel early enough in the morning to get you to the first interview with time to spare.

In this case, scheduled for the mid-morning interview, it got later and later, and the media host who was supposed to pick me up at the hotel had not arrived. I realized that if she did not arrive in the next five minutes, I would have to find my own way to get to the television station, prep for the interview, maybe get makeup on, and be in the chair on the set, ready to go live, with only a small amount of time to spare. I decided to give my driver five minutes to arrive before I took matters into my own hands.

As I paced the sidewalk outside my hotel, the five minutes went by, and still no driver. So I waved down the next cab I saw and jumped in, telling the driver that I needed to get to a television station fast, and I gave him the name of the station and the address.

The driver turned in his seat, smiled a big smile, and said something in a language I did not understand.

I repeated the call letters of the television station, and the station's address, and repeated that I had to get there fast.

Nodding and smiling the driver pulled out and sped off—in the wrong *direction*.

I knew it was the wrong direction because I had been able to see the television station's transmission tower in the distance from my hotel room. I immediately told the driver that he was making a mistake, and from his very first response—he was still nodding and smiling—I realized that he did not have the slightest idea what I was saying.

I began pointing frantically out the back window of the cab, trying to explain the image of a television tower that I could see plainly in the distance. I went through all the verbal techniques that insensitive Americans use when they're trying to be understood by someone who doesn't speak English. First, I repeated the words, "Turn around," several times, repeating the words louder each time I said them. Then I repeated the words again, this time enunciating each syllable very slowly, like you would do when you imagine teaching language to children.

Along with that, I was using sign language, drawing a circle in the air with my pointing finger, meaning to turn *around*, each time ending up pointing to the distant, receding television tower in the rear window. I was trying to be calm and deliberate, and utterly clear when I repeated "Tel-e-vision tow-er, tel-e-vision towwwerrr," again and again, trying to make the shape of a television transmission tower with my hands, pressing them together, pointing them upwards while at the same time I swirled them around and around in the air and thrust them toward the back window of the cab. It must have looked I was crazy. If I weren't desperate, it would have been really funny.

Finally, with a huge grin, the cab driver began to nod enthusiastically, then suddenly made an illegal U-turn in the middle of four lanes of traffic and shot off in the direction of the television tower. When he did this, I was less afraid of the swerving traffic and blaring horns than I was of the fact that I was scheduled to be on the air for a super-important interview, on live television, in less than five minutes.

With me doing a lot more pointing and repeating words, we somehow actually got off the main highway, through the streets, and frantically made our way to the television station. When we came screeching in to the security gate entrance at the side of the station, I had less than 60 seconds before I was supposed to be on the air. As I rolled down my window in the back of the cab, the security guard took it all in instantly, and the first thing he said was, "Are you Dr. Helmstetter? We're ready for you."

What consummate professionals these television people were! As I scrambled out of the cab, the guard grabbed me by the arm and pushed me through the security entrance door. Just inside the doorway, running down the hallway toward me, was an engineer with a portable headset and microphone, and as we ran together toward the main backstage area, the engineer was putting an earphone in my ear and briefing me at the same time.

"The show host is sitting on the set right now," he told me, "next to an empty chair, introducing you. We've told her you're on the way. They've got the camera on her only, and she's the person you can hear talking in your earpiece right now."

Still running up the long back hallway, and then making our way through the backstage area of the live studio set, I could hear my interviewer introducing me, and then she was talking to me, having a "conversation" with an empty chair that the viewers at home could not see.

With the camera only on her, *for nearly a full minute of live air time,* while I was running through the back hallways on my way to the set, the host had been talking to an empty chair.

And then I was pushed into my seat on the brightly-lighted set, my collar was straightened, the engineer jumped out of the way,

145

the camera moved back, and there I was sitting next to the show host who was chatting with me, saying, "*. . . and it's great to have you with us, Dr. Helmstetter,*" as though we had been sitting together the entire time.

So with the cameras now on both of us, I turned to her, hoping to look completely calm and relaxed, and responded, "It's good to be here."

A few seconds later we went to a break, and the moment the cameras were off, I heard the engineer shout "Holy s…!!"

I looked at the host and we both shook our heads, amazed that it had worked. The host let out a long sigh of relief as she said, "That's live television."

Of all the many interviews in all of the cities and states I traveled to, there were only two of them that came anywhere close to what I would call "negative interviews." At least, that's the way they started out.

Among all of the television and radio stations I appeared on, there were very big stations and also small ones. The people at the small stations were always gracious and courteous; it was sometimes the bigger ones that thought they were special.

I remember one radio station, a large station in Minneapolis, Minnesota. The talk show host who was going to interview me had apparently not learned manners when he was growing up. He may have been trying to be an early Howard Stern, or maybe he just thought it was okay to make fun of someone. Maybe he was just a bully.

On the morning I was on his radio talk show, it was mid-winter, and freezing in the Twin Cities. I remember that when I was brought into the studio, I couldn't help but notice this host had a deep tan, a kind of greenish-orange, unnatural tan. I don't think I would have even noticed his obvious tan-in-a-bottle if it weren't for his "I'm a big guy" attitude. Everything about him seemed kind of false.

Anyone who knows me would say that I would be the last person to criticize or find fault with someone else. And that's true. But when I walked into this particular radio studio I felt like I was in the presence of a people predator, someone who preys on others—in this case, as a radio talk show host—for his own benefit.

We chatted for a few minutes before we went on the air, live. As we did so, he was mostly asking questions about the book I was there to talk about, but there was something suspicious about his demeanor—there was even something wrong with his smile—and my antennas went on high alert.

After a commercial or two we were on the air. And when the red light went on in the studio control room, in the flicker of a moment, this radio talk show host morphed into his true self. His odd smile turned to an evil sneer, and there was no warmth in his voice at all when he started with his first question.

"Dr. Helmstetter,*"* he enunciated with too much emphasis on the *Dr.* part of my name. And he continued, now holding up my book, and singling out from its 255 pages a single sentence, saying, "I hope I'm not taking this out of context . . ." (As if *any* single sentence from an entire book would not be out of context!) Then he said, "It says here, that '*What happens to you next will depend on what you do next.*'" And then he looked directly at me and said, *"Are you talking to idiots here?"*

And after a short pause, I said, "Do you mean *in general* . . . or *right now?*"

I love the Midwest; I was born and mostly raised there, but another radio talk show "attack" host, happened to also be in the Midwest. This one started his live, one-hour talk show by saying,

147

"My guest today is one of those guys who is going to try to sell you the Golden Gate Bridge."

The talk show host, who had not read my book, and had no idea of what the book was about, was setting me up for a negative interview, and was grandstanding to get an easy, deriding response from his audience—at my expense.

We were going to be on the air, live, for a full hour, so I did the most practical thing a guest on a talk show could do with a host that should have been doing something else for a living. I remembered that in grade school our teacher had taught us that when we weren't supposed to speak, we would turn an imaginary key in front of our lips, locking them, and making it impossible for us to speak. I figured that grade school was about the emotional level that the talk show host was at. So that's what I did. I locked my lips.

After he had introduced me with the absurd opening comment that I (his guest) was going to try to sell his audience the Golden Gate Bridge—and I realized that this was not a real interview, with an actual intelligent human being talk show host—I held one hand up in the air in front of him, between our two microphones, and I pressed my forefinger and thumb together, like I held an imaginary key, and brought it to my lips and turned the key and locked my lips. I then looked directly at him, shook my head very slowly from side to side, meaning *"I'm not going to say a single word during the entire show,"* and sat back in my chair, my lips sealed, waiting for him to talk to himself for an entire hour on live radio.

When the talk show host realized that I meant it—I wasn't going to talk—he suddenly looked shocked, panicked even. He stuttered something, and then immediately went to a commercial. As soon as we were off the air while the commercial was playing, he tried to apologize by saying he was only kidding, and he was going to do a great interview. After a time, the interview did go as it should have, but that good interview was the result of my understanding, beneficial heart, and not because of any redeeming qualities on the part of the host.

There were other times when I had to do something special to help get an interviewer on track. On one occasion I was ushered onto a television set where I would be interviewed by a Ms. Williams.

When I got there, Ms. Williams was already sitting in her host chair, and while I was getting seated, I said, "Hello Ms. Williams, I'm Shad Helmstetter," and put out my hand.

She ignored my hand, and turned away as she said, "I know that," with an unmistakably disinterested, superior look on her face. She was either not a nice lady or she was having a very bad day.

So to lighten her up and hopefully save the interview I said, "I thought we could take a moment and I could answer any questions you have," hoping that would warm her up.

But she was cold as ice as she glared at me and said, "That's what the interview is for!"

Wow, I thought, *I'm about to go on live television, and talk about my book about being positive, with a television host who hates life. I need to fix this.*

So I waited until the producer said, "Sixty seconds, Ms. Williams," indicating that we had just one minute to go before we went on the air.

I looked right at her, with a serious look on my face, and said, kind of rushing the words, "I thought you would want to know how I came up with the idea of self-talk."

And without pausing I went on, "It all started very late one night, at about two o'clock in the morning, when I was driving by myself on a dark country road in the middle of the desert in New Mexico, and I saw what I thought at first was a just a bright star in the sky, but then it started getting brighter and brighter, and it kept coming closer and getting bigger, and then it got even closer, and

149

all of a sudden it was huge and bright and it was right above my car, and everything around the car was all lit up, like daylight, and then I must have blacked out or something because all of a sudden the bright light was gone, and I was about sixty miles farther down the road and two whole hours had gone by, and when I woke up, I realized . . . I had been given . . . *the secrets of the universe.*"

And just then the producer said, "Ten seconds, Ms. Williams." Ms. Williams was looking at me with her eyes wide open, almost in shock, realizing she was about to do a live news interview with someone who was completely crazy.

And then, just before the two-second signal, I pointed my forefinger at Ms. Williams, like I was holding an imaginary gun, and pulled the trigger, and quietly said, "*Gotcha!*". . . and smiled.

I've never seen a news anchor suddenly look more relieved than when Ms. Williams realized I had only been kidding, and I wasn't really crazy. The ice melted, and it turned out to be a fine interview.

Then there was the time I was on such a hectic, over-scheduled media tour that I actually collapsed from exhaustion just after being on the Oprah Winfrey show.

I could feel the fatigue and exhaustion building each day, but I had a schedule to follow and a dozen airline tickets in my briefcase; I didn't have time to stop or rest. I often thought that the people who scheduled the tours had never been on a media tour themselves, and never realized you shouldn't schedule an author on "Good Night New York," and the next day on "Good Morning San Francisco."

The problem wasn't mental stress—it was physical exhaustion. The next thing I knew, that I could remember, was that I was in a hospital room with tubes in me. The wonderful thing was that later, about ten o'clock that night, after I had gotten stabilized and had rested, the television in my hospital room was on and I got to watch the rerun of the Oprah Winfrey show that I had appeared on earlier that day. The nurses, who were down the hallway, were watching the same channel, and within minutes I became a celebrity, while lying in a hospital bed. Nurses came in to check on me so often I couldn't get any sleep.

I must have been okay, because my normal sense of humor came back, and while I was lying there watching my heart monitor with its steady beep, beep, beep, I wondered what would happen if I hit my chest with my fist. I tried it, and the heart monitor went crazy. So I did it again. In seconds, first one, then two more nurses rushed into my room, expecting to find me in the middle of a seizure or something, but I was lying there smiling, and just said "Hi!"

When I told the nurses what I had done to get the monitor to go crazy, the senior nurse made me promise to never, ever, hit my chest like that again, and told me that it had almost given *them* heart attacks.

So I waited until they had all left my room, and had gotten settled back to normal, and I was watching the heart monitor again, and I had an idea. I then gulped in the biggest, deepest, longest breath of air I could . . . and then I held it . . . and held it . . . and held it . . . until once again, the heart monitor alarm went off. I know I shouldn't have done that, but it was fun smiling again and saying "Hi!" when they all came rushing back in.

The next day I was released from the hospital, and I got on an airplane, and went to the next city on my television tour. It had been another wonderful Oprah show. And I would be willing to bet that none of the other guests that had been on her show that day had a story that good.

Most of the interviews themselves were great interviews, with good hosts, good questions, and when they took phone calls, great listener call-ins. Some of them stand out because they were unique among interviews, and you would never expect to see another interview like them.

An example of this is one of the times I was scheduled to appear on CNN. Even the letters "CNN" at that time represented such an icon of news, and the power of the media, that if you were invited to be interviewed, not just for a two-minute segment, but for two or three longer segments, that would be Nirvana for any author, or for any publisher wanting to promote a book.

The interview was on a Friday night at 10:00 p.m. Major opportunity. Top exposure. Huge results if I did it right.

But on Thursday morning, the day before I was supposed to appear on CNN, I woke up with laryngitis, and I couldn't talk. So, being appropriate, I called the producer, who was in Atlanta, and told him in a hoarse whisper that I had laryngitis and he might have to find someone to replace me.

But surprisingly, he reassured me, and he told me to fly to LA and show up as scheduled. "You've gotten good ratings in the past, the audience likes you, and we want you on. We'll take care of everything," he told me. "Don't worry about a thing."

The producer was referring to some kind of internal rating system they had, where they could tell from the audience's response how well the guest was doing. A low rating was 1, and the highest rating you could get was a 20. In the past I had gotten a 16, so that was a good score and high enough to be invited on again.

I knew CNN could do some amazing things, but I didn't think they could cure laryngitis. However, I agreed to do it, and on Friday night I showed up at the LA studios.

I was ushered into a large, mostly empty, and mostly dark television studio and seated at a table on the set. Off to the side in front of me was the television monitor where I could see the two co-hosts who were actually in CNN's studios in Atlanta, who would be interviewing me via split screen. In the center of the floor was a giant camera on a dolly, and there was an engineer behind the camera.

Before we went live, an assistant inserted my earpiece—called an IFB—so I would be able to hear the producer and the two hosts. As soon as I got the IFB in place I heard the producer saying hello to me and asking me how I was doing.

"I'm okay," I whispered, still barely able to talk.

"Well, don't worry," he reassured me again. "We've got you covered."

What they did next was very smart. First, the technician who had wired me with the IFB put a high-sensitivity microphone right up under my chin, closer to my mouth than usual, so it could pick up my slightest word, instead of down on my lapel where the small microphone would usually have gone. Then a stage hand brought in steaming cups of hot tea with lemon juice and honey—the same potion my grandmother would have used for treating laryngitis—and put them on the table directly in front of me. Then they raised the camera up so the cups couldn't be seen.

The idea was that when the camera was off me and on the two hosts in Atlanta, I could take a sip of the hot tea and honey.

Then I heard the producer speaking in my IFB. "Here goes," he said. The red light on the camera came on, and we were on live in front of millions of viewers. What followed was the most interesting interview I have ever been on.

I could see the male host on the monitor as he introduced me, and when the camera turned on me, I smiled and nodded my head enthusiastically. Then the female host immediately said, "Dr. Helmstetter, you say in your latest book that what parents say to their kids actually gets programmed into their brains, isn't that right?" to which I nodded, again, enthusiastically.

Without a pause, the male host chimed in, saying, "Well, if that's the case, then it sounds like as parents, we really need to be careful of everything we say to our kids. It looks like we might be programming them in the wrong way without even knowing we're doing it," to which I smiled and nodded again even more fervently.

With comment after comment, perfectly passed from one to the other, those two brilliant hosts conducted an entire interview with *themselves.* When the camera wasn't on me, I'd sneak my sips of hot tea and honey, and when the camera was on me I would enthusiastically smile and nod my head, trying to get a whisper out as loud as I could.

When it was finally over, and the red light went off, the producer said to me in my IBF, "How do you feel now, Dr. Helmstetter?"

"Fine," I whispered.

"Well, you did great," he said. "You got an 18."

For the next interview I did at CNN some months later, this time my voice was back to normal. I reported back to that same huge, dark studio. I was seated at the same table, saw the monitor where I could see the hosts in Atlanta, got miked up and my IFB put in my ear, and waited for the red light to show on the camera that was on the large dolly about fifteen feet in front of me. The camera dolly had wheels on it so the camera could move easily with just a little push from the engineer. The red light went on, the interview started and we were underway.

Everything was going fine when, halfway through the interview, I noticed an odd thing happening. I could see myself on the television monitor, and I noticed that my head was slowly starting to move sideways, off the screen! I glanced back at the man operating the camera, leaning against it with one foot on the dolly, and I realized *the camera man had fallen asleep,* and as he leaned on the camera, it was slowly rolling to the right!

So I started to slowly slide out of my chair, sideways, keeping my body straight, moving sideways to the table, so my head stayed in the center of the screen—while the background graphic, a color photograph of the nighttime skyline of Los Angeles, was slowly moving behind me.

Then suddenly the producer yelled into the IFB and the cameraman woke up, jumped, and immediately jerked the camera back into place. As he did, I quickly slid back into my seat, staying centered on the camera screen the whole time, and the show went on.

At home, the viewers had seen the nighttime skyline of Los Angeles moving behind me and suddenly jerk, and shake, with no warning or explanation. The next day I heard that the CNN switchboard got flooded with calls from viewers who thought that during my interview, there was an earthquake in Los Angeles.

What I learned:

I cannot imagine an environment in which you have to be more on your toes, and more on top of your game, than in dealing with the media, especially when you're being interviewed. Many careers have been made or lost on a person's ability to dance deftly with the media.

My first—and lasting—takeaway from all those interviews I made it through is that it is not about the person who is interviewing you—it's about your audience, the people who are watching or listening. Remember them, every moment, and speak to them, and you won't go wrong. (If you try to "please" the host or the interviewer, you can get tripped up, often.) It's the audience that rules. Speak to *them.*

Chapter Twenty-one
On the Road Again

Because one of the things I decided to do in my life was to speak to audiences about self-talk, I had to make the choice to love travel. That can be tough to do. There have been times when I almost never saw home. One year, with an over-booked speaking schedule, I was home a total of sixteen days. I don't know of a city of any size in the U.S. or Canada that I haven't been in, most of them many times. And, in the mix, I also traveled to speak in a lot of places in other parts of the world.

So right from the start, I had to make the choice to make peace with travel, to make it okay, especially airline travel—lost suitcases, frantic, overcrowded airports, missed connections and all. If I didn't have a positive attitude about it, I know I could never have done it.

I vividly recall one time an accountant who was doing my books, and reading over the long lists of hotel stays and expenses, somewhat naively complained that he and his wife only got to stay at a nice hotel maybe once every year or two, and I was staying in hotels month after month. He was remarking on all of the hotel expenses and what he saw as the flamboyance of it all.

If only he knew. Non-stop traveling, living in hotel rooms, is not a vacation; it's an endurance test.

My accountant had never arrived at a hotel in a downpour at midnight and stayed up until two in the morning setting up chairs in a hotel ballroom for a seminar that would start at eight the next morning. He had never arrived at a hotel at six in the morning expecting to do a seminar for three hundred people in that hotel two hours later, only to find that there had been a mix-up—the ballroom had been rented to someone *else*—and three hundred people were about to start showing up with no ballroom and no seminar to go to! If they found you, they would want to lynch you. (It worked out, but only because of help from the hotel staff. We did the entire seminar in the huge hotel lobby.)

On one occasion prior to a seminar at a hotel in Phoenix, Arizona, the seminar staff was excited to see that the huge ballroom was filling up with people, and we would likely meet our target of 850 attendees. That was the maximum capacity of the hotel's largest ballroom. But the attendees just kept pouring in, non-stop. When over 1200 people were trying to pack their way into the room, the fire marshal arrived and said we were over the limit and they couldn't all fit. So we opened all of the large double doors along the rear of the entire ballroom, and we did the seminar to a packed room—*and* to packed hallways.

On another occasion, we were scheduled to hold a seminar in one of the most beautiful hotel ballrooms in Los Angeles. The high ballroom ceiling was aglow with dozens of beautiful crystal chandeliers, each of them dangling dozens of long blade-like icicles of glass shards. Stunning.

But at 4:30 a.m. on the morning of the seminar, a 6.7 level earthquake struck Los Angeles, and we were shaken out of our beds and had to go to the streets in our jeans or pajamas until the "all clear" alarm was sounded.

When we finally entered the seminar ballroom later that morning, the icicle chandeliers on the ceiling were still swaying and tinkling dangerously from the aftershocks. I could only imagine hundreds of people sitting for three or four hours looking up as the sharp glass icicles swayed above their heads.

No seminar. We put a sign on the door, with no disrespect intended, which read, "The Shad Helmstetter "Self-Talk for Success Seminar" has been canceled due to God."

On another occasion that nature dropped in, I was in Kentucky and preparing to speak the morning after a night of heavy rain that had poured down on the city. I was scheduled to speak to a large audience of teachers and educators, and was about to receive the state's Kentucky Colonel award, when a huge gaping split in the roof broke open, and hundreds of gallons of water poured down from the roof into the amphitheater all around me. I remember telling the audience when I spoke—it was a miracle I was still dry myself—that the night before I had prayed for God's bounty to be showered upon us from above, and that in the future, when I prayed I would be more specific.

One seminar was an especially important event because it was the first self-talk seminar presentation by a man I was grooming to be a stand-in for me—if I was ever not able to make it. So on this occasion I would not be presenting the seminar; my stand-in would, as a test.

I stood inconspicuously at the back of the packed ballroom, attentively listening to his opening presentation, and as he spoke, I was beginning to feel uncomfortable; his charming wit and normally outgoing personality were missing, and his delivery wasn't up to what I thought it would be. I could also sense that the audience wasn't responding.

Then, ten minutes into the seminar, the fire alarm in the hotel sounded, and a blaring voice over the PA system alerted everyone that we all had to leave the building until the building was checked and cleared. So everyone rushed out to the hotel parking lot. Twenty minutes later the "all clear" was announced and we could return to the seminar. When I got back into the seminar room I had pangs of compassion for my stand-in speaker. Several *hundred* people had left the seminar room when the fire alarm sounded— and only *nine* of them returned.

Later, I would find other people who could stand in for me. In time, with the help of the Self-Talk Institute, I would train many people who now deliver the self-talk message flawlessly.

But curiously, as good fortune would have it, in all of my public speaking years I never missed a single seminar or speaking engagement. I was never out due to illness, bad weather, or missed airline connections. I feel very fortunate about that. (I did live with a sometimes over-active concern for catching colds. And because in a public speaking environment you shake a lot of hands, I always carried hand sanitizer, and I also washed my hands a *lot*. On second thought, maybe that's why I never missed a seminar.)

This period of public speaking and presenting self-talk seminars did not last for a just year or two; it began in 1982, and other than a few quiet times along the way, it has been a part of almost every year of my public life. I knew that was the job, I knew it had to be done, and I was thankful for the opportunity to do the job in the best way I could. Speaking to audiences was an important part of getting my message out to the world. Whatever that took, I was dedicated to doing it.

My speaking years have been made up of two kinds of speaking. The first kind of speaking is self-talk seminars, with the most popular of these being seminars on "Self-Talk for Success," or "Self-Talk for Weight-Loss." The other kind of speaking is for groups and large business organizations, with a lot of invitations to speak to network marketing organizations.

Fortunately, I was saved from the difficult job of finding speaking engagements. Speaking is a good field, and most speakers work very hard to develop a list of clients whose companies or organizations will invite them to speak. But because I also produced my own public seminars, I was saved from having to find clients.

By the time my first book was becoming popular and I was appearing on the Oprah Winfrey Show and news channels like

159

CNN, I was able to fill my own seminar rooms with four or five hundred to a thousand or more attendees, and although it took work and dedication, I did not have to worry about finding the next audience. But that, too, would have its ebb and flow.

I remember a time when I was tired out from doing public seminars, and I had "gone to ground," my style of stepping back for a while, and waiting for the universe to present itself. I do not believe in trusting in fate only, and doing nothing, but sometimes *waiting with intent* is doing *something*.

At the time my wife and I had found a small rustic writer's cottage on the water on Mobile Bay in Mobile, Alabama. Anytime I needed a rest, I would write, and that's what I was doing. Finances were very tight—I had no public speaking events scheduled—and it was definitely chicken salad days, and we had to watch expenses very carefully.

I had come to the conclusion that because it had been quite a while since my first, and most popular, book had come out, and since I was not touring, that by now most people had forgotten about me. And that was my mood. Not dejected. Just realistic. My time, I realized, may have come and gone.

Eventually, I began to recognize that my boyhood dream of changing the world might not happen after all. I didn't want to give up, but even though I had done my best, I had not been able to reach the rest of the world that I had wanted to reach with my message, and I started to think I would just have to let my dream go.

But I was never a quitter, and even though it seemed to me that my efforts may have been in vain, and there was no longer an audience for my message, something inside me told me I shouldn't give up—even though, in some of the darker days, I was tempted to quit.

And then one day the telephone rang. It was a call from one of my book readers who asked if I would speak to a group in Atlanta

160

a few weeks later. I asked how large the group would be, and the caller told me it would be a good-sized group. I told him I would speak to his group, but that I would not be charging for my speaking. I had the belief then, and still do to this day, that you should give before you receive. The people inviting me to speak would pay for travel and lodging expenses for my wife and me, and I would be able to bring self-talk audio cassette programs that I produced, and those would be offered for sale.

On a whim, I had enough of those self-talk audio programs produced to exactly fill a van, the van that I would rent for my wife and me to drive to Atlanta to give my talk. Then, the day before the speaking event, we loaded the van with the albums of self-talk programs, and headed for Atlanta. The event hosts would have a table at the back of the room somewhere, for people who were interested in buying the self-talk programs. The next morning at eleven I would be introduced, walk on stage, and give my talk. Whether we would sell any self-talk cassette programs, I had no idea, and I realized that I may be speaking to an audience where no one knew me.

At ten o'clock the next morning I decided to go down to the convention floor an hour before my talk, to size up the room, and meet with the event hosts who had invited me there to speak.

When I got to the very long, two-story escalator that would take me down to the convention floor, I noticed that the entire area surrounding the bottom of the escalator was filled with a massive throng of people. I stepped onto the top escalator step, and when it moved downward toward the crowd, they started to cheer.

About halfway down, I looked behind me to see who they were cheering for. There was no one there. And with complete surprise, I began to realize they were cheering for me. By the time I got to the bottom, I was engulfed in a multitude of book-reading fans. A thousand of my books were being waved in the air.

161

Everyone wanted to get an autograph and talk. Apparently, some people still remembered me.

People who know me well know that I don't buy the whole idea of the glamor, or of being in the spotlight, and that I know that it's all created, and little of celebrity is actually true. Celebrity, unless you're Albert Einstein or Helen Keller, is usually fabricated and created for the purposes of business or the media.

So when I descended the escalator to the cheering crowd of a thousand or more event attendees, I only remember thinking, "I'm glad I accepted this gig." It took me almost an hour to get into the hall so I could speak.

I spoke for ninety minutes to an audience of four or five thousand people, the self-talk product table was swamped, and the next morning my wife and I drove home, with, other than our suitcases, a completely empty van. I don't talk about money and finances much, but that one day provided enough income to get us through the next few months.

Fortunately, before we got to the end of those months, the phone had started to ring again, and for the next twenty years it never really stopped ringing. The public hadn't forgotten, and I was back on the road again.

I am certain that in life, for the most part, you create your own luck. Your thoughts create your destiny. But now and then we are smiled upon by angels or guides that, at least for a time, take the boulders and the ruts out of the path we have been set upon, and life just *works*.

For three decades of time in my life, I stayed on the road, speaking about self-talk. Or, if I wasn't on the road at the moment, the next year would find me there again.

When I was on tour conducting the public self-talk seminars that I produced, because of the number of people attending and the number of tasks there are to handle at a seminar, I often traveled with a small staff of four or five trusted team members.

When the team and I would have to be at one city to give a seminar on a Saturday and at a different city on Sunday, if the two cities were within driving distance of each other, we would drive between them instead of flying. With the endless hassles at airports, we would rather do anything than fly.

I had gotten the idea that renting a passenger van would be a lot less expensive than flying, and I then discovered that having a limousine drive us was also a lot less costly than flying. Traveling in a limousine can sound like putting on the Ritz, but the limo drives were often for two hundred miles, usually very late at night and into the early hours of the morning, and we often only got to our hotel and asleep at one or two in the morning. So with a hired car and driver we could all rest some during the ride to the next city, instead of dealing with the problems of airports and flying.

Plus, I enjoyed the positive camaraderie of the staff. Having sandwiches with friends at midnight in a limousine under a starlit sky in the middle of Texas isn't a bad way to travel. I remember one time I was just sitting back and dozing during the ride, and I happened to wake up and look out the window, just as a sleek, black limousine was pulling past us. Half asleep and harkening back to the poverty programs of my youth, I thought, "There goes some filthy rich person." I had forgotten, for the moment, that my team and I were also riding in a limousine.

What I learned:

If you want to test your left-brain, detail-oriented, problem-solving skills, while you hone your right-brain attitude and people skills, go on a speaking tour. Every one of those skills can be challenged every day . . . and it won't let up until the tour is over.

I often noticed that I always agreed to a brutal speaking schedule when I had been *off* the road for a while, and was completely rested. I would think about that while I was in the middle of what seemed like the endless tour I had too easily agreed to do.

But I will say this: I absolutely *refused* to complain—at any time. No matter what the problem was, I dealt with it and looked for the good within it. That doesn't make me a saint—being "up" was essential. After all, how could you complain, be down, or have a bad outlook, and then walk on stage and talk to an audience about how to have a positive attitude?

What happens when you practice positivity in the face of adversity is that things generally end up working better. (The brain actually gets wired that way.) I knew that from my research, but being on endless speaking tours for what seemed like endless years, proved it. I am eternally grateful that living in the positive really works.

Chapter Twenty-two
Helping One-On-One

I first had an idea about helping people individually, one-on-one, fairly early on in my journey. In 1972, it was just a small idea, but it was an idea that would grow.

My idea was that it might be possible to help people discover the answers to the important questions they had about themselves or their futures, if you were to ask them exactly the right questions, and in exactly the right order.

And then, according to my idea, you would have to let the person answer each of those questions—without any criticism about anything they said, and without guiding or suggesting the direction or tone of their answers.

If you did that exactly right, I proposed, you could help people replace uncertainty, fear, or other emotional responses, with more logical, less emotional answers to some of life's most important questions. And they would discover the answers for themselves; it would not be an outside therapist or counselor that would suggest what they should do next.

I believed that for this idea to work, the "coach" would have to avoid using any of the popular tools of the trade of counseling or therapy; that is, they could not influence the subject in any way, beyond the simple asking of each of the questions, without opinions, advice, or other feedback.

At the time, the term "life coach" had not yet been invented. People were accustomed to therapists dealing with psychological problems, and there were also popular seminars in which people were guided in ways to unlock their inner giants and take personal control of creating their future realities. But the idea of talking to a personal "life coach" for forty-five minutes or an hour by phone each week would not even begin to become popular until another thirty years in the future.

So, without any guidance or history to go on, I decided to test my idea on my own, and conducted my first personal life coaching sessions. I invited clients to come to my home in Cupertino, California, and spend two days over a weekend sitting in comfort in a beautifully-appointed living room with plush white carpets and an ebony studio grand piano. For an intense schedule of many hours each day, I asked them questions (that I had pre-written), one after another, pausing infinitely long between questions, allowing them to think, and then rethink, and then to answer the question.

During the entire session time, I didn't offer a single suggestion or point of advice. I simply wrote their answer to each question on a large pad of paper on a standup easel. When they were ready to give their final and best answer, I wrote it out on the pad where they could read it.

I then asked the next question, said nothing, and waited for them to answer. I tried to show no facial or body language signs of agreement or disagreement, approval or disapproval; I just waited, without comment, for each answer, and wrote it down.

This process, as I had designed it, lasted for hours. During that time, in a logical, building order, the questions guided the client to his or her own conclusions. And the process worked. When the clients reached their own conclusions, they were incredibly clear. The hard-won conclusions they reached were powerful, and they were life-changing. By reading and reviewing the answers he or she had given, the client knew *exactly* what to do next, and why.

During this process I had not given the client a single sentence or word of advice. I just asked the questions, kept my mouth shut, waited endlessly, wrote down the answers word for word, and let the real conclusions and the real answers come to the client, *from* the client. In every case, without exception, every time I "coached" a client in this way, the results were remarkable.

I had found a way to help people find themselves—define their goals, and set a clear course for their futures—with no gurus or external guides to tell them what those answers should be. The clients were finding the answers for themselves.

Over time, I refined the questions and worked to make the sessions less grueling, and as more clients sat in that comfortable chair and answered the magic questions, I could see that the process was working. People were coming to brilliant conclusions, answers were coming from their own mouths (and their own hearts), and they were often answers that were completely unexpected.

During the time in my life that I was conducting the life coaching sessions, I knew the idea had great merit—but I had many other responsibilities, and I continued to stay busy in the rest of my life. After having successfully tested the concept, a number of years would pass before one-on-one life coaching would re-enter my life.

It reappeared later, when I was focusing almost entirely on writing books and doing radio and television media appearances on the subject of self-talk. The concept of my approach to personal coaching had never left my mind; it was a powerful concept, but I'm a person of focus, and at the time, in my work, self-talk was my primary focus.

Then, one day in Scottsdale, Arizona, I walked into my favorite restaurant, and something happened that brought all of my enthusiasm for my coaching system back to front and center.

In the restaurant I ran into one of my early coaching clients whom I hadn't seen or heard from in several years. It was a man who, at the time I coached him, had been a very successful—but very unhappy—businessman with problems in his work and in his marriage, and he was frustrated by the fact that he was not doing what he really wanted to do in life.

Now, several years later, after an accidental meeting in the restaurant, the businessman glowingly laid out for me the story of his life following the coaching sessions—and told me how his life had changed in every positive way; marriage, career, purpose, and personal fulfillment—he had put it all together. He thanked me and thanked me, and all the while I was remembering back several years to his coaching sessions, and that he had found all the answers by himself. I hadn't said a thing or offered a *single* piece of advice—I had just asked the magic questions.

Following that, as synchronicity would have it, I began hearing from another, and then another, of my early life coaching clients, and all of their stories were remarkable; every one of my clients' lives had leaped forward, often in wonderful, positive new directions, following the coaching sessions. In each case, they had found the answers they had been looking for, and in each case, because of the coaching format we had followed, they had found their own answers by themselves.

When I reconnected with these clients, and heard their amazing successes that they attributed to those hours we had spent together, it was clear that the coaching process had worked for every one of them. It was changing their lives with the right interconnection between just two people, one-on-one.

It was then that I decided to find a way to teach this coaching method to others, but it would take several more years before I could devote my time to developing a complete life coaching program that virtually anyone could be trained to use.

My final solution was to write a word-for-word life coaching manual (a binder about three or four inches thick) of fifty-two coaching sessions, one session for every week of the year. What I did was write out the exact questions that I would ask the clients if

I were there, standing in front of them, writing their answers on an easel pad as I had done years before.

But now I broke the questions into specific categories, specific wants and needs and problems and goals that people have in their everyday lives. Those client needs became the fifty-two life coaching sessions that I wrote in the *Life Coach Manual*. That manual became the guide that my future life coach students would be trained to use with their own clients.

I also got rid of the one thing in the process that could make it difficult to do. Instead of requiring the coach and client to be sitting together in the same room, my updated system would work better by phone than in person. That turned out to be a positive game-changer. It meant that I could teach people to use the coaching system, and the people they were coaching could be anywhere in the world.

I will add that much later, after testing this idea with many coaches and many clients, I now believe that almost no life coaching session should be conducted in person, with the two people, the coach and the client, sitting in the same room, looking at each other. I remember all too well how, when the client was sitting in front of me, I had to play automaton, a robot in every word or inflection. I didn't want to do anything the client could read falsely or get the wrong impression from—like the look on my face, or some body posture or motion I might unconsciously be making. (When a client is talking, the coach might unconsciously shake their head thinking, "That's wonderful!" While meanwhile the client, seeing only the shaking of the coach's head assumes they are showing disapproval, feels criticized, and subconsciously reacts accordingly.)

After a lot of time and a lot of work in continuing to develop and perfect the life coaching system I had first practiced in 1972, I eventually founded the Life Coach Institute (in 2001) so that I could teach the system to anyone who wanted to become a successful life coach.

Many years ago, sometime after I had first begun using my early version of the coaching system with clients, but before I founded the Life Coach Institute, I was working for a company that published self-improvement programs. I continued to be very excited about my idea that you could use a coaching system like this to help people find answers and do better, and I decided to tell my employer about my idea. I thought that he would naturally recognize its potential and perhaps brainstorm creative possibilities.

But instead of supporting the idea, my boss told me that I had no right to do what I was doing, that there were no college courses in the kind of thing I was talking about, no one else was doing it, and that it was a silly idea that would never work, and shouldn't work, because I had no right to do it.

Years later, when the Life Coach Institute, the organization I founded to train coaches, became a major leader in the life coaching field, and the Institute had graduated its first thousand trained and certified life coaches in countries across the world, I did not call my old employer and share the moment with him, or tell him he had been wrong. There would have been no value in doing that, and it would have been unkind. But I do think he could have used the services of one of my graduate life coaches, who help people create a belief in the positive, and find a future that works.

Once the Institute was up and running, I began training new life coaches in person, in groups of fifty or sixty at a time. The Institute first sponsored training classes in different cities throughout the U.S., but after two or three years, the classes were moved, seamlessly, to the internet.

The result is that there are now thousands of trained and certified life coaches (from many countries) who know exactly the right questions to ask, in exactly the right order, and they are taught how to coach without giving advice, without giving personal opinions, and without telling other people how to live their lives. But they're very good at helping clients find their focus, set goals, find the right solutions, overcome the challenges, and take action steps to reach any goal they set.

The reason I was interested, years ago, in the new idea of personal coaching, was born out of my personal goal of helping people improve their lives. Later, when I began training other people to become life coaches, I was working on the same goal—but I had expanded the goal to helping people help *other* people.

I believe that if I hadn't chosen that particular purpose in life, and decided that *that* would be my path, I wouldn't have thought of "coaching" others, one-on-one, at a time when no one else I knew of was doing it. I wouldn't have developed a process that would work universally, and I would not have carried the idea to its logical extension of teaching other people to become life coaches—and do the same thing I was doing.

Now, decades after I conducted my first coaching sessions, life coaching has become very popular. There are life coaches everywhere, and they come in all styles. Many of them (those who were not trained by my institute), sometimes heavily flavor their coaching sessions with personal opinions and advice. But I would be careful who you listen to. Other than parents teaching their children, I have never met a *single* person in my long life who had enough intelligence and wisdom to tell someone *else* how he or she should live his or her life. And yet, there are well-meaning coaches who are doing that every day, floating personal opinions cloaked in life coaching advice.

I like all of those who are helping people. But as you can imagine, I've never liked the idea of life coaches dispensing opinions. (Opinions on how you ought to run your life should be left to family and friends, who will give you their opinion whether you ask for it or not.)

What I learned:

My greatest take-away from my work in coaching is that nothing back then, in the new world of life coaching, was an accident, not even at the beginning. I didn't start with the goal of founding the Life Coach Institute and training several thousand coaches. It was entirely driven by a single, earlier choice I had made when I was setting my course in life—to help people improve their lives. That choice created the future. Everything that followed was the logical result of that one first step.

I also learned that I absolutely *love* life coaching. There is almost no greater feeling of accomplishment than to watch a person—the one you're coaching—literally change and grow, and they're doing it themselves.

I still love the whole idea of life coaching today, even though my world has changed, and with only a few exceptions, I haven't been able to work one-on-one as a personal coach.

I've often said to my family and friends that I would still love to coach individuals, even though, in a very practical way, my time is better spent reaching more people by talking to audiences or writing books. But I *love* life coaching! That's where I took a significant step in my journey some forty-plus years ago, and the joy of helping someone week after week, and watching them grow, has never gone away.

Maybe, if I ever even *think* about retiring, or semi-retiring, that's what I'll do; I'll coach.

But then, I never think about retiring.

Chapter Twenty-three
Walking Around the Tree

One of the simplest, and yet most helpful, strategies of my life came from a problem I wanted to solve when I was living at my writer's cottage on Mobile Bay on the Gulf of Mexico.

When I was sitting in the cottage's small study, with its old fireplace and its glass-paneled French doors, looking out onto the patio and beyond, I would often look out toward the water to gain inspiration. It was being able to write on the water that had drawn me to that cottage in the first place.

But there was a problem: from my writing study I couldn't really see the water, only a small part of it. Much of the rest of the waterscape and horizon were almost completely occluded by the heavy low-hanging boughs of a large old pine tree that stood on the bank of lawn just above the sea wall that dropped to the water below.

To create the unbroken view of the water that I wanted, I would have to get a very tall ladder and climb high up the trunk of the old pine tree, high enough to be able to reach the lower branches with a saw, do some heavy sawing, and get rid of all of the branches that were spoiling my view.

But getting high enough up the trunk of the tree was a problem; the branches that needed cutting started at about fifteen feet and higher off the ground, and I didn't want to buy a ladder that I would probably need to use only once. I also didn't want to hire tree cutters to come out to trim just one tree; not remove it, just cut off the lower branches.

So what I decided to do was to *walk around the tree*. Once or twice a day, for the next three days, when it was time to take a break from writing, I would go outside, down to the sea wall, and walk around the old pine tree and look up to where I wanted to get to. From ground level, I would study the tree from every side, looking at every possibility.

Then, on the third day, after walking around the tree again, and looking at it once more from every side, I had it. I knew the answer.

With the answer in my mind, I went out to the garage at the front of the house. After a few minutes I came back out with two eight foot sections of two-by-two-inch boards, a saw, a hammer, and a pocket full of four-inch nails. I went back out to the pine tree and sawed the boards into 18-inch sections to make steps. I nailed the first step into the tree at about knee high, and the second one about a foot above that, and the third one another foot above that one.

I then climbed up on the first step and nailed two more steps above the first ones. I kept doing that until I had a series of steps that ran all the way up to where I needed to stand to saw off the lower branches which had been blocking my view. Instead of buying a ladder I would never need again, I had nailed a ladder of temporary steps into the tree.

Once I stood at the top of those steps, I was high enough to be able to saw off, one by one, each of the branches that had obstructed my view of the water.

When I had finished sawing off the branches, I climbed back down the steps I had nailed into the tree, and removed each of them one by one from the top down, until I was back on the ground.

Finally, I removed the last step from the tree, carted off all of the branches, took the boards I had used as steps and my hammer and saw back into the garage, went into the house, sat down in my study, and looked out the window.

What I saw now was an uninterrupted horizon of shoreline and water—just what I had wanted to see—with the entire bay in front of me. Then I got back to writing the chapter I was working on.

That simple experience reaffirmed to me that when I'm dealing with a problem, the first thing to do is study it, "walk around the tree," and look at it from every side, so that every creative solution will start to become apparent.

Some people may have looked at that same pine tree and immediately said, "It's easy. Just make your own ladder by nailing steps up the trunk, and take the steps down again when you're finished." But I didn't see that solution immediately. I had to walk around the tree. And I learned something permanent from that exercise. No matter what the problem, I still do the same today. No matter how difficult the problem is, I walk around it until I have it figured out.

It was at that same writer's cottage on the water that I encountered another problem that was new to me. The lawn and home overlooking the bay stood ten feet above the water, and protecting the land from the waves and water was an old seawall. It was this seawall that presented the problem; it was old, and it was beginning to break down.

The bottom part of the wood plank seawall needed to be repaired. But that section of seawall was several feet under water. In this case I couldn't exactly "walk around the tree," but what I could do was walk along the top of the seawall and study it, as I thought about what needed to be done. I needed to nail some heavy wooden planks into place deep under the water to keep the water from eroding the soil behind it and washing my yard away.

After a couple of days I came up with a solution: My list of materials to repair the seawall was: six wooden planks, one heavy hammer, two dozen four inch nails, *and my scuba gear.* For the next few hours I felt like a Navy diver, working underwater on my own seawall. Problem solved.

How we solve problems has always been an important adjunct to my research and what I have written and taught. That's because how we solve problems is always based on our mental programming; it's why some people are good at solving problems, some people aren't, and still others don't even try—they live in a mental world of victimhood and feel powerless to do anything about anything.

Dealing with problems has also been important to me because it is such an important part of setting and reaching goals—something that I believe to be essential to any real achievement or self-actualization in life.

What I learned:

At some point in time, I think quite early on in my life, while I didn't cherish having problems, I began to look forward to solving them. And that happened, undoubtedly, because of the absolute love of creativity that got programmed into me when I was growing up.

If everything is "perception" (which I believe it is), then most problems we face are great or small depending on how we choose to look at them.

When you have a problem, study it. Walk around your own tree, and watch yourself doing it. In time, for me, doing that became a habit—one of the good ones.

The concept of "walking around the tree" is a way of addressing a problem, right up front, by saying, "I can do this. I can figure this out. I can solve the problem." That's a great way to look at challenges. It's also great self-talk.

Chapter Twenty-four
What Else Do I Do?

When I meet people who know that I write books and speak to audiences, I'm sometimes asked, "What else do you do?"

I've always thought that a person should have many interests in life, and that avocations are as important as the person's primary job or vocation.

Some of my interests, beyond reading and learning, often have something to do with architecture or design. I believe that in one way or another, most of my life has been about form and structure, design and balance, shaping things to fit. I certainly have done that in working with human behavior and personal growth. And that same desire to help people create balance and form in their lives has also been an important part of the other areas of my own life.

I might have been an architect, or a design engineer. I work with stained glass as one of my serious hobbies, but I might have worked in stained glass professionally. I could have been a professional photographer. I might have been a sculptor. Or I might have directed movies. Those thoughts are not casual, pretending thoughts; they are what I believe about me. If I had chosen to follow any one of those other paths, I would have excelled in that path.

One of the most important messages I have written to the readers of my books is that you are not limited to what you do—you are limited by what you *believe* you can do and what you *choose* to do. And I have often made the choice to allow my own belief in myself to come alive, and to expand my life.

As an example, when I live in the appropriate environment, when I have the space, I design and build remarkable things—summer houses would be a good example. I lived for several years in Virginia Beach, Virginia, in a house that was built over two hundred years ago, in 1794. I loved that home. When I walked up the staircase to its second and third floors, I would often be reminded that there were little children playing on those same stair steps before Thomas Jefferson was president.

During the time my wife and I lived there, we brought the old home back to life by completely restoring it to its original self—not like an old museum of a home, but a home that made you feel in every way that you had stepped back in time and were actually living in that house in the past—like when it had been newly built, two hundred years earlier.

To bring that home back to life, we brought the original heart pine flooring back to its warm, rich, gleaming amber hue. We redid walls, fireplaces, two-hundred-year-old hand-milled cedar siding (we had new cedar siding hand-milled to the identical shape and specifications of the original cedar siding), a full, new shake shingle roof, ceiling moldings, and chair railings—we brought it all back and we made it live again.

The home stood on ten acres of land, and on the lawn near that beautiful old house, there was a large open area, by the rose garden, that seemed to call for a gazebo. So I decided to build one. Not just a normal gazebo, but something that Thomas Jefferson himself might have designed. I based the design on Jefferson's popular octagonal architectural motif, and drew plans that would make it eighteen feet in diameter, with an elegant domed roof.

By the time I had finished designing it and having it built, it was actually a summerhouse and not a gazebo. It was air-conditioned and completely enclosed, with large multi-paned windows all around, glass French doors front and rear, an outside balcony on the back side, and a huge, stately staircase leading up to another balcony on the front.

Inside, its beautiful woodwork included layers of heavy, deep moldings surrounding the domed ceiling, indirect, hidden lighting in the dome, and a large, colonial brass chandelier in its center. For a time, a studio grand piano stood on its amber-toned heart pine floor. (To lay a heart pine floor in the summer house that would be true to the original heart pine flooring that was in the main house, I found a lumber company who milled the wood for the flooring from old heart pine logs that were pulled up from the deep cold water of river bottoms where they had sunk and rested for a century or more, so the flooring in the summerhouse would be old, like the flooring in the main house itself.)

When it was finished, the entire summerhouse structure stood like a gleaming white and crystal Faberge gem. And I surrounded it with an antique-brick patio, with tall, stately white lanterns on each of the eight corners of the octagon courtyard.

The total number of bricks—combined, between the bricks in the courtyard surrounding the summer house, and in the courtyards on each side of the big house—was 10,000, and I chose to lay all of them, one by one, by myself, by hand.

I also laid an antique brick walkway from the summerhouse to the big house, and then designed an arched awning that would cover the entire walkway, so even on a rainy day or night you could walk from the main house to the summerhouse without getting rained on.

At night, with all of the antique lanterns and the summerhouse's chandelier and sconces turned on and dimmed to a soft glow, the summerhouse became a beautiful shimmering jewel of light. I thought it was exquisite.

Apparently other people also thought so, because the year the gem-like summer house and the rest of the restoration was

completed, the city of Virginia Beach, Virginia voted our home the
"*Home Design of the Year*"—and it had been built in *1794*.

In any project that I do, I accept credit for its design, and for
successfully bringing it to life. I'm not doing that in any immodest
way. In each case it is my intention to create a work of art. And
when that's your intention, you've got to know when you're
getting it wrong, and you've got to know when you get it right.
When you get it right, say so. Learn to recognize the feeling that
tells you when it's working, so that next time you can get it right
again.

With the summerhouse and old original house standing
nearby, I could not afford to get it wrong. As owner of that
property for the time I lived there, I felt that my role was as its
steward; adding to its beauty and quality, and making sure that it
would be there for another hundred or so years to come. That's
how I looked at it. That was my goal, so that's what I did.

Some time later, we moved to northern Florida, on the Gulf of
Mexico, to write. After trial and error searching, we eventually
found a home in the country that also had pastures and a barn
with stalls for my wife's two horses. One of the reasons I loved
this property when I first saw it was that a small, rushing creek ran
through it, and beyond the creek was a small lake on the other side
of a rise of land. To me, that rise of land next to the lake was the
perfect place for a gazebo.

If you guessed that I decided build another architectural
construction, and view it as a piece of art, you are correct.

This time I built an over-the-water deck pavilion, one like you
might find in The Great Gatsby—decks and white railings and
lantern posts and a dock on the water—and in the center of the
large, multi-leveled pavilion deck, like the top of a beautiful white
wedding cake, a gazebo. Stairs and banisters lead down from the
pavilion on the lake to an arched bridge over the bubbling creek
and an elevated wooden walkway that leads to our home. I write

there, from time to time, in that beautiful gazebo pavilion on the water.

I believe that life is a canvas, and you can paint on that canvas whatever you choose. I've held that belief for many years, and it has always been one of the focuses of my life.

For a number of years, in my thirties, when I was in my corporate life, working as the director of creative marketing for the electronics and music corporation I talked about earlier, I began to explore a lifelong interest in Egyptian art and architecture. When Tutankhamen's tomb relics went on tour and the world discovered the exceptional artistry and craftsmanship in those irreplaceable works of art, I marveled at them. In all of Egyptian art, I was enamored of the sculptures and the gold statues, but especially the carved stone "stele"—the wall carvings that adorned so much of Egypt's past.

I wanted to have life-sized Egyptian carvings on the walls in my home. But that idea presented two problems. At the time, I couldn't afford even the replicas that were for sale, and besides, I didn't think most of the replicas, even those from well-known art museums, looked "real." They looked like plaster replicas, not like the real thing.

So I thought about it, and I decided I could do better myself. I would find a way to make something look like perfectly carved sandstone, and I would create Egyptian-appearing artifacts with ancient hieroglyphics carved into them, and I would put them on the walls in my home.

At the time, I was living in a condo in Memphis, Tennessee, about a mile from Graceland, Elvis Presley's home. He was still living there at the time, and now and then, on my way home from my regular job, as I passed by, I would see Elvis out front by the large, wrought-iron gates with the singer's guitar-playing images on them, riding his horse or spending time at the gate for signing

181

autographs. (I never stopped. I didn't think he would want my autograph, anyway.)

I had figured out that my ancient Egyptian hieroglyphic sandstone artworks would have to be carved in something I could manage, like high-density polystyrene, and if they were covered with the right combination of sand and stone-colored pigment, they should transform into something that would be virtually indistinguishable from solid, ancient carvings in stone.

I had temporarily converted the dining room in our condo into a "sandstone application testing room," and I still remember so vividly, late one night, after working for weeks to find the right formula, I finally found it.

It was very late, just after two in the morning, when I was testing a new coating solution on one of the carvings I had made, that something magical happened. While I stood there, drying the surface of the carving with my wife's hair dryer, the stone carving on the table in front of me suddenly came stunningly, incredibly to life. Clearly stone, carved, ancient, and completely and accurately Egyptian.

I stood there for a long time, just looking at it. As I stood there in the middle of the night, transfixed, the "stone" tablet that had come to life in front of me defied one to think anything other than *real*, and very, very old.

Eventually, after more work perfecting my formula and technique, I hand-carved a large, four foot by eight foot, framed, museum-like set of wall panels of Egyptian stele, carefully carved to be old-looking—with real looking cracks carved into the stone——and it looked as though I had taken this huge Egyptian artifact directly from a tomb in Egypt and brought it into my home. I loved it. And I knew it was amazing.

Everyone else who saw it also thought it was amazing. Within a year I had started a company called Artifax Corporation to manufacture ancient stone artifacts, and also to license the rights to the process I had developed, to other manufacturers. One of the company's first orders was from the manager of promotions for a company that produced music tapes. One of the artist's albums they wanted to promote had a cover that depicted the famous NASA photograph of the footprint of the first man on the moon, and we used the Artifax sandstone process to reproduce hundreds of lifelike replicas of the famous Neil Armstrong footprint for music store displays.

Following that, a company in the business of making merchandise displays signed a licensing agreement to use the Artifax process in making a variety of realistic stone-like in-store displays.

Significantly, I received a check upon the signing of that agreement, and my wife took a picture of me holding the check the day I received it. It was uniquely special to me because the check I was holding was for a thousand dollars *more* than my entire annual income that I was paid from the company I was working for at the time. One idea—creating Egyptian art for my home— had just earned more than working for someone else for an entire year.

After first beginning to draw as a kid, and then learning oil painting, mechanical drawing and architectural drawing in high school, I continued to always do some kind of art. Like a lot of people who learn to be creative, I went through different phases of expression: drawing, painting, sculpture (a life-size statue of the Buddha sat in the corner of our living room next to a gold-leafed statue of Tutankhamen), architecture, stained glass, and so on.

When I was creating the self-talk concept and began writing books, I assumed the job of creating the cover designs for most of my books, and also the ads that were placed in industry magazines like *Publisher's Weekly.* I also began to create all of the newspaper advertising for self-talk seminars, advertisements that would appear in newspapers everywhere.

For a very long time, even after I had created artwork for dozens of book covers and ads, I was hesitant to publicize the fact that I was most of the "design department" for the companies or institutes I worked with. But when I needed to get a specific idea across, I found it faster to create the ad or the cover design myself, and I knew that if I was doing the graphics, I would get exactly what I wanted.

I'm sharing my focus on my interest in design and form here because that interest is integral to everything I do. Things like shape, color, composition, relationship, strength, pattern, and balance, are all things you could ascribe to art and design. But they are also all things you could ascribe to almost any area of life that you wanted to understand or improve. And all of them are part of a rhythm, an endless series of patterns in our lives that are made up of infinite vibrations and frequencies—the energy of life.

There is a sacred geometry to the universe itself. Like the ratios of the "Golden Section," the well-known mathematical ratio that we find in every area of life from the petals of a flower, to the proportions in the face of DaVinci's Mona Lisa, to the form of the human body, to the spirals of distant galaxies—everything we see in our lives that we explore can be brought down to its form and balance. Understanding that is the essence of art.

The more a person knows about these sometimes invisible balancing and shaping rules of life, the more that person will be prepared to see the broadest and most in-depth picture of life itself. That's why every great civilization that has ever lived is remembered not only for the fairness of its justice, but for the perfection of its art and the endurance of its architecture.

This is not a book that is written to give advice, but I would suggest one thing. If there is someone in your life, like a child, who shows an interest in art or form, encourage him or her. Seen or unseen, art and form are very big parts of the patterns and balance of our lives, and an important part of making our lives better.

Beyond designing and creating things, I was programmed from childhood to have an insatiable appetite for learning something about just about everything. That interest never went away. It's like the childhood game my siblings and I played called "Battle of Wits." Only today, the game is played in the midst of life itself.

I also study, and watch very carefully, what is happening in humankind's venture into space. Along with having many other interests, I am particularly fascinated with the exploration of space, and what that will hold for the human species and for Earth itself.

Unlike some, I do not think for a moment that we are alone in our universe. I am certain that not only are we not alone, but also that we have no *idea* how vast life is throughout the heavens, and how closely we may be related to cousins from there.

As a species, we have always been incredibly myopic, never looking much farther into the distance than watching for the next enemy who may be coming over the closest hill. Because, with our own first, meager steps into space, that perception appears to be beginning to change, we may be about to experience the greatest evolution of thought that humankind has ever had to face.

When I'm not busy challenging my mind with dealing with the necessities of life or designing or creating or building something or learning something new or pondering the questions of the infinite universe, I am thinking about what I'm going to think about next. Each night, after I say my nighttime prayers, with my head on my pillow, in the dark, I choose what subject I'm going to think about as I go to sleep.

It's a busy mind, I know. And you might wonder, "Why not give it a rest?" I might have, especially as I have gotten older. But at that same time, as I started to get a little older, I began to do research into a book I was writing called *The Power of Neuroplasticity*. In that book I write, among other things, about what keeps the brain young, and what mental activities grow new neural pathways in the brain. With what I learned from my research, I am completely happy continuing to "think" as a hobby—it is clearly the smart thing to do—when I could so easily have been doing nothing, watching television, or letting my brain sit idle.

I wrote in *The Power of Neuroplasticity* that there are certain activities you can engage in that stimulate the brain, grow new neural connections, and improve both your mental and your physical health. One of those brain-enhancing activities I discovered was archery.

I had not picked up a bow (as in bow and arrow) since I was twelve years old, but my research suggested that it would be a healthy and mentally stimulating thing to do.

So I purchased an adult starter bow and a target, and I shot my first arrows from a safe, close distance of thirty feet. I knew from brain research that the more I practiced, the more I would be rewiring my brain with new neural networks for everything I was doing with archery—focus, spatial distance relationships, muscular control and precision, mental calm—and determination to have the arrow reach its goal. I did all of that, going through the routine with every careful arrow I shot. But in addition to that, I loved it, and I kept at it.

In a short time, I acquired a more professional bow, and with my continued practice, I continued to get better. I practiced every day, and I watched and measured my progress.

I was buying more targets and placing them at greater and greater distances away. I kept at it until I was confidently sending five carbon fiber arrows into a tight grouping into the center of a target a hundred feet away. And then it was a hundred and fifty feet, and then two hundred, and eventually, the holy grail of archery, 70 meters (229 feet, 7.906 inches) away, the Olympic archery target distance.

I hadn't necessarily planned to gain the skill to enter Olympic archery competition; but I loved getting there. What it did for the wiring of my brain was wonderful.

One evening, as an example, during the time I was practicing archery, I was boiling eggs for a salad I was going to have. The eggs were resting on the counter top in our kitchen, when one of the eggs rolled off the counter. Without flinching or without thinking, my left hand dropped down and caught the egg in mid-air. Two days later, once again boiling eggs, another egg rolled off the counter, and once again my hand caught it in mid-air.

When I was catching a baseball, I stopped having to look where the ball was coming from, and when it would hit my glove; my glove was just there, catching the ball, without my conscious mind having to find it. My days of perfecting my archery were having an auxiliary effect in the rest of my life; I was fine-tuning all of my senses with a sharper degree of awareness and physical acuity that my archery practice was wiring into my brain.

Today, on any given evening, if I'm not somewhere by the water writing, or on an airplane traveling somewhere to speak, you will often find me where my wife and I live in the country, with my bow and a quiver of arrows, aiming at a target so far in the distance that you have to use sports binoculars to see if the arrow hit its mark.

The whole idea of archery, and hitting the target, is our best-known metaphor for what I have spent so much of my life studying and writing about: setting goals and hitting the mark. I think about that when I'm in the archery field, and have just reset the targets a few more meters farther away. That's what progressing in life is about. And that's how working to get better actually happens.

Whether it is getting better at archery, shooting arrows at a target more than half a football field away, or doing something entirely different, like bringing stone carvings of Egyptian artifacts to life, or studying the spiritual side of life, or exploring the unknown meaning of our participation in the star-filled galactic neighborhood we live in, I am certain that I, like so many of us, have utilized only a fraction of the capabilities that we were born with in the first place.

I'm still working at it, and doing my best to get better in every way that I can. But when someone asks me today, "What else do you do when you aren't writing or speaking?" my answer is *"Everything."*

What I learned:

When I chose my life's work, and dedicated myself to following it, I also knew that by making that choice I could be limiting my future to one very small part of life. That kind of extreme focus can create success in a single pursuit, but it can also create over-focus, a kind of fanaticism; which leads to imbalance, and an extremely narrow view of life.

So to counter the limited, but intense, focus of my life work, I learned that I also had to practice balance, and not only be open to a broad range of interests, but to explore them, learn about them, be able to talk about them.

An example of my perfect picture of the Renaissance person lifestyle would be to sit down next to anyone, a complete stranger, on an airplane, and no matter who it is, spend the entire flight talking about that person's life, what he or she does for a living, asking questions, being genuinely interested, and learning things I had never known before.

Chapter Twenty-five
The Music of My Life

I have mentioned elsewhere in this autobiography that music, in many forms, has been important in my life—including how I grew up with music, and how I write all of my books listening to specific selections of music.

But there is another, important part of the chapter to the story of the music in my life.

Sometimes it seems as though we are given gifts, for no apparent reason—that we can't always see at the time—to help us on our way. In my life, one of those gifts has been a very special piece of music.

If someone were to ask me what has most influenced the way I think, or the way I look at life, I would first point to the kind of creative thinking I was raised with. But to tell the complete story, I would also have to reveal the role that has been played by this one piece of music.

This part of the story of my life may be unique in that *I have listened to one piece of music, almost daily, and often, as I slept at night, for more than fifty years.* If I could easily verify this, it would make the pages of the *Guinness Book of World Records* for the number of times an individual has listened to a specific piece of classical music. As astonishing as it sounds, I have listened to this one piece of music more than *three hundred and fifty thousand times.*

The story of my special music began when I was in Cuba, when I was spending long days and nights translating critical messages from Spanish to English for the government. I didn't drink any alcohol, so while my teammates were decompressing at the local pub, I was in my barracks cubicle, usually reading, or writing letters to my wife, and almost always listening to classical music.

Then, late one night, I was listening to a short-wave radio broadcast, recording music off-the-air from the BBC, when I happened upon a piece of classical music I had never heard before. This amazing musical work captured my attention instantly. It was riveting in its depth of expression. It went directly to both my mind and my soul. It had a haunting theme, almost dark, but also uplifting, ethereal, mystical, and to me, very, very beautiful.

I had recorded the piece—it was only about fifteen minutes in length—so I was able to play it back on the tape recorder that stood on the writing table next to my bed. I had headphones connected to the tape player, so I could listen to music while I was going to sleep, without bothering my three teammates who shared the same cubicle in our barracks.

The first night I went to sleep with the newly-found "mystical" music playing in my earphones, I experienced the most relaxing sleep I had had in months. So the next night, I tried it again; when I went to bed, I put my headphones over my ears and listened to the same, hauntingly beautiful musical piece—and once more, the same thing happened—I slept another night of the most peaceful sleep I could remember.

Just having that particular piece of music playing in my earphones as I drifted off to sleep took me to a place of complete inner peace and well-being. It spoke to me in an unusual way; it seemed timeless, and it seemed to lift me out of my body in a transcendental, almost spiritual way.

But that was just the beginning. Thereafter, for the entire time I remained in Cuba, every time I lay down to sleep, I put my headphones over my ears, pushed the "play" button on my tape recorder, and listened to "my music."

Even though I was very familiar with most of the classical music works that were popular at the time, I had never heard this piece before; I had no idea what the name of the selection was, or who wrote it, and I had no good way of finding out. (This was long before there was an Internet, and there were no other classical music buffs among the service members who lived in my barracks.)

While others around me were finding their lives filled with a lot of stress, and, with nothing but visits to the pub to help them escape for a few hours, my own anxiety and stress had amazingly dropped to something below zero—as each night I listened to that music. For the rest of my time while I was in Cuba, every time I went to sleep, I slept with that special music playing in my headphones—and I slept the sleep of angels.

When I eventually returned to the U.S., I brought my "mystery" music home with me. I still had no idea what the name of this music was, who composed it, or who had performed it. All I had was a tape recording that I had made from an almost ethereal—faint, mystical, ghost-like—overseas broadcast I had recorded in the middle of the night, in Cuba. But even after I returned home, I continued to listen to the music I had found.

Finally, after a time, I was able to discover the name of the piece and the composer who wrote it. Some of my readers will not be surprised to learn that the music that had brought me to such a deeply calming, introspective place in my mind was a popular English work entitled "*Fantasia on a Theme of Thomas Tallis*," written by the composer Ralph Vaughan Williams. (Since then, I have always just referred to it as *"Fantasia."*)

I was then able to order an original recording of the LP record, which I also recorded on tape so I could listen to it at night. (I even made a special "under pillow" speaker so I could listen throughout the entire night.)

Since that time, *Fantasia* has always been with me. I have continued to listen to its mystical, ethereal tones at night, and even during the day when I'm reading, and want to relax. Without

191

exception, each time *Fantasia* plays, my mind settles down, and it finds an immediate sense of peace and calm. In later years, after I discovered the idea of listening to recorded self-talk, if I wasn't listening to self-talk as I went to sleep, I was listening to *Fantasia*.

In time, I added other Vaughan Williams pieces to my nightly playlist. (One of them, *The Lark Ascending*, is one of the most poetically visual and beautiful pieces ever composed, and it sometimes vies for first place with *Fantasia* on my nightly listening list.)

But to this day, when I listen to *Fantasia*, my mind immediately goes to a higher, otherworldly place—a place that is not mundane, or fraught with the problems of the day. As the first notes of the music begin, within moments, my awareness transcends the ordinary, and gives me a view of life that comes from an almost timeless perspective. It lifts me up, and holds me outside of the moment, showing me a view of the past, the present, and the future in a way that rises above everything that is earthly and temporal—and places me outside of the bondages of an earthly "now."

Some say the sounds of Tibetan bells are healing and spiritually centering. It is because of that same quality that I mention this music here. The Vaughan Williams music I have listened to, almost every day (or night) of my adult life, has undoubtedly played a significant role in my thinking, and in fact, my view of life, all these years.

While so often the world around us was unsettled, when I listened to *Fantasia*, my world would always be brought back into a safer, more reasonable place, out of the chaos, into an almost spiritual, monastery-like place in my mind—a place in which I have always found comfort, clarity and endless perspective.

Looking back on it now, without any doubt, this unusual music that I listened to, the music that led me calmly into my sleep each night for over fifty years, has played a profound role in influencing my thinking and my picture of life—and almost every action I have taken. It placed my life, for years, in a space that reminded me of the task I had come here to do, and always let me know that that's why I had come here in the first place.

Technically, neurologically, I understand that listening to the music of *Fantasia*, and similar works, has done what many popular pharmaceuticals attempt to achieve with pills and medications, chemically, in the human brain. But by choosing music instead of medication, I avoided the harmful side effects of the medications; I also used my brain's natural processes to create a natural, more healthy, deeper state of mind, without having to use pills or medications to take me there. (I'm in no way suggesting you should stop taking your medications and start listening to *Fantasia*. Talk to your doctor.)

At best reckoning, and as impossible as it seems, it actually *is* over three hundred and fifty thousand times, usually playing quietly throughout the night while I'm sleeping—for over fifty years—that Ralph Vaughan Williams' *Fantasia* has played in my life.

(The math is: If you listen to one piece of music that is repeated four times an hour for six hours, that is 24 times a night. If you listened to that piece of music for a minimum of just 300 nights a year, you will have played that one piece of music 7,200 times in one year. If you keep playing that same piece of music 24 times a day (or night) for fifty years, you will have played it 360,000 times.)

There are gifts that are given to us to uplift our lives and make them better, and this music, that I first heard on short-wave radio one night in Cuba, on the BBC, when I just happened to have my recorder turned on, is one of those gifts.

What I learned:

I've often thought about what my life would have been like if that uplifting, *transcending* music had not been a part of my life all these years. I suspect that my world might have been quite different—certainly less peaceful—and I would have been far less mindful, day after day, of the higher purpose of being here in the first place.

And I'm very glad that *Fantasia,* in particular, has been here with me.

Chapter Twenty-six
Sartebus and Kim

There are times I find that the best way to get a message across is to write a parable, a story that is universal, so every reader will understand what I'm trying to say. I'm including one of these parables here—one that I created for a book that I wrote over twenty years ago. I'm including it because it sums up what much of my life's work has been about.

An interesting side note about this parable is that a few years after I first published it, it made its way onto the internet, and different people who are complete strangers to me translated it into different languages, and almost all of them present the parable as having been written hundreds of years ago. Although I actually wrote this parable in 1995, it does have a message for all time, and whoever the strangers are who carried this story forward, thinking it came from antiquity, I thank them.

Here is the parable of *Sartebus and Kim*:

There is a story of an old man and a young boy who lived in ancient times. The old man was named Sartebus, and the boy was named Kim. Kim was an orphan, living on his own, making his way from village to village in search of food and a roof over his head. But most important of all, even more than his search for a full stomach and a comfortable dry place to sleep, Kim was looking for something else—he was searching for a *reason*.

"Why," he wondered, "do we travel throughout our lives in search of something we cannot find? Why must things be as difficult as they are? Do we make them so ourselves, or is it just meant to be that we should struggle as we do?"

These were wise thoughts for a boy as young as Kim, but it was just that kind of thinking that caused him to find along the way an old man, traveling the same road, who, Kim thought, might help him find the answers to his questions.

The old man was carrying on his back a large, covered, woven basket that appeared to be very heavy, especially for someone as old and weary as he was. When they stopped to rest beside a small brook along the road, the old man wearily settled his basket on the ground. To Kim it looked as though the man carried all of his worldly goods in that one basket; it seemed to be much heavier than even a much younger, stronger man could carry very far.

"What is it in your basket that makes it so heavy?" Kim asked Sartebus. "I would be happy to carry it for you. After all, I am young and strong, and you are old and tired."

"It is nothing you could carry for me," answered the old man. "This is something I must carry for myself." And he added, "One day, you will walk your own road and carry a basket as weighted as mine."

Over many days and many roads, Kim and the old man walked many miles together. And although Kim often asked old Sartebus questions about why men must toil as they do, Kim did not learn from him any of the answers, nor could he learn, try as he might, what treasure of such great weight was in the basket the old man carried.

Sometimes late at night, at the end of a long day's journey, Kim would lie quietly, pretending to sleep, listening to the old man sorting through the contents of his basket by the flickering light from a small fire, and talking quietly to himself. But in the morning, as always, the old man would say nothing.

It was only when Sartebus could walk no more, and he lay down to rest for the last time, that he told young Kim his secret. In their last few hours together, he gave to Kim not only the answer to the riddle of the basket he carried, but also the answer to why men toil as they do.

"In this basket," Sartebus said, "are all of the things I believed about myself which were not true. They are the stones that weighted down my journey. On my back I have carried the weight of every pebble of doubt, every grain of the sand of uncertainty, and every millstone of misdirection I have collected along my way. Without these I could have gone so far. I could have lived a life of the dreams I saw in my mind. But with them I have ended up here, at the end of my journey." And without even unwrapping the braided cords that bound the basket to him, the old man closed his eyes and quietly went to sleep for the last time.

Before Kim himself went to sleep that night, he untied each cord that bound the basket to the old man and, lifting it free, carefully untied the leather straps that held the woven cover in place, and lifted it aside. Perhaps because he had been looking for an answer to his own question, he was not at all surprised at what he found inside. The basket, which had weighted old Sartebus down for so long, was empty.

What I learned:

I discovered when I was young that it can be a difficult task to teach the notion that life, and how we see it, is an illusion—that it is only what we perceive it to be. These days, with philosophy and physics beginning to come together, the message may be getting clearer; but the story of Sartebus and his basket helps to simplify the message even further: Everyone carries a basket. It is up to each of us to decide what is in ours.

Chapter Twenty-seven
The Newborn Nursery

If someone were to ask me whether I would live my life over again, knowing the time and the dedication it would take to find my purpose, and then attempt to live it out, I would only have to think of a newborn nursery, and the precious infants who begin their life's journey there, to know my answer: Yes, I would do it all over again.

To me, one of the most magical places in the world is a hospital's newborn nursery. I've had the opportunity to visit those sacred places many times—and it's always wonderful. But to me it's more than just being able to visit the newborn infants in their first days of life; it's imagining the amazing futures they have. Their futures are virtually unlimited.

When you're standing in the visitor's area of the nursery, you look through the viewing window and you see those wonderful miracles of life in their little bassinets, wrapped in their swaddling blankets, and you can't help but see the limitless opportunity that lies in front of them.

Imagine standing there, and right in front of you, through the viewing window, you see two bassinets, side by side, and in each of them, there is a precious little infant. Each of those infants was born to excel, to live a life of incredible fulfillment. If they're awake, and their eyes are open, you can almost see them searching, looking into their futures, waiting to live a life that is filled with endless, positive growth and purpose and happiness. Born with talents and gifts and unending qualities, their whole, amazing, wonderful lives await them.

It is so clear to me that each of us was created to succeed. No one is created to fail. We are all designed to live a life with a potential far beyond what most of us ever imagine.

But then something happens. Not everyone succeeds.

Think, for a moment, of the most successful person you can imagine. It could be anyone who you believe to be a successful person—not just financially—but in every way. This would be a person whose life moves in a positive, upward spiral, filled with achievement and happiness. This is someone you might like to know well or spend time with, or emulate in some way. This is a success; this is a person whose life *works*. Get a picture in your mind of who that successful person is. And when you see that person clearly, imagine that he or she is standing in front of you.

Then, while that successful person is standing there, think of someone who is on the *opposite* side of life—someone who is *failing*.

(When I think of someone who is failing, I immediately think of someone I knew of years ago, who left home as a teenager and ended up in the world of drugs. If his parents could even find him today, it would probably be in an alley somewhere, and he probably wouldn't even recognize his parents if he saw them, because of the drugs and distortions in his brain.)

But whoever comes to mind when you think of someone who is failing at life, imagine that that person is with you now, and is also standing in front of you.

Now, standing in front of you, is one person who is succeeding at life, and one person who is failing at life. When you look at each of them, and understand their journey, it will be obvious that they are worlds apart in their lives—one is happy and successful, and the other is unhappy and failing.

I have often thought about this picture, and it always brings up the same question: *Why is the one person successful, and the other person is not?*

The answer is: It's not luck or destiny, and it's not an accident; it's their *programs*. It is how they got programmed—after they were infants in the newborn nursery.

It's the messages that got wired into their innocent, receptive, eagerly waiting brains—by the people who gave them their programs. It was their parents and their teachers and their friends and their experiences. Word by word, sentence by sentence, mental picture after mental picture—even things like: "You'll never amount to anything," or "You're going to be fat like your mother's side of the family," or "You're so stupid, can't you do anything right?"—got wired into their brains.

In time, the programs they got repeatedly, became the self-talk that would direct their lives—and that self-talk created their futures. Whatever gets wired into our brain, we end up living out.

What is astounding to me is that these two people standing in front of you now—so utterly different in their lives—could have been the same two precious infants who were in front of us in their basinets in the newborn nursery just moments ago, their entire lives in front of them, with their eyes open and searching, ready to live a future of unlimited promise. And it is entirely possible that these two people—so different now in almost every way—could have been born in the same hospital, in the same hour, on the same day—both created to succeed, and with the same potential in front of each of them.

When anyone has wondered what kinds of things motivated me all these years, it has been pictures like those of the precious infants in the newborn nursery, with their entire lives in front of them.

What if we could change what happens next?
That is what has motivated me.

200

What I learned:

All I have to do is to think of those infants, and countless others like them, to realize that it was all worth it.

Every step I have taken in my efforts to inform people about the way their brains really work, and how to rewire their brains for better results, I saw as a step in the right direction.

My prayer is that those steps have lived up to the dreams of that young boy in the wheat field—the one who started it all, and hoped for so much.

Chapter Twenty-eight
Starlight

Imagine seeing the sky at night when you're six years old. That is when my real journey began. That's about the time when I was beginning to think about things outside of myself.

Imagine seeing the universe above and around you in that night sky, with such great depth and endlessness that you could get lost in it, and if you stayed there long enough, rising up into that eternal infinity of starlight, you would come back to Earth excited and frightened by what you had seen, filled with both intense exhilaration and fear.

When I first looked at that sky, really looked at it and thought about it, I had gone outside of our home one crisp, brilliantly clear night, and on that night I lay on my back in the grass and just looked *up*. I had seen that clear, bright night sky many times before, but that night I really looked at it, really *saw* it. For the first time, it made me more excited about what was out there than I had ever experienced. And it also made me more terrified than I had ever been.

On a clear night, the sky above my childhood home was blessed with a lack of man-made light that could have obscured the view. Living in a very small town in the middle of the countryside, a town with few streetlights, all of which were canopied, there was nothing between me and the immense, overpowering beauty of the stars in the Milky Way above me.

I can still remember how my stomach began to tighten with a strange sense of unrecognizable fear as I forced myself to lie there on my back, moving upwards into that dazzling array of stars and galaxies above me. I could actually feel myself lifting up, almost as though I was flying upwards into the firmament, bright, and brilliant, a universe of light that was welcoming me *home*.

It might be an odd thing for a six-year-old kid to lie on his back in the grass and lose himself in the stars, and feel a powerful magnetic feeling that pulled him upward, and be aware not only of the unknowable and unimaginable depth of the star field above him, but also aware of a kinship with them that was calling him home. But that's exactly what I felt. Earth was temporary; the stars were my home.

After that night, the notion of identifying with the heavens on clear nights was so powerful a pull to me that I would often go outside my home at night, lie down in the grass, and look up into the sky until I felt the depth of space lifting me up, and I could once again ascend into its "welcome home" embrace. I would do that even when it started to get frightening, when it scared me as I rose up into it.

What frightened me—and sometimes terrified me—was that in church each week I was beginning to learn about the infinite endlessness of "eternity." I was learning in Sunday school that if we were good, we would go to Heaven and live there *forever*. That was tied to *infinity*, which meant a really, really, endless forever.

Put the picture of infinity and an "endless forever" together with lying on your back and moving upwards into an endless nighttime field of stars that also went on into eternity, and you could suddenly realize that there was no end to anything. And you were a child with no power over the immensity that was engulfing you.

I remember clearly, after lying on my back gazing into the heavens on one of those bright starlit nights for perhaps an hour or more, finally standing up, getting up from lying in the grass, ready to go back into my home and rejoin the safety and the normal life that waited there.

But just before I turned to go into the house, I stopped and looked up again. And when I looked up, my spirit rose, easily and naturally, up into the stars, like an angel winding its way to Heaven, and I was home. And then, with a "real" life to live, I came back to Earth, went inside the house, and I was home there, too. Two homes. Very close. Very real. Both of these places in my life were home.

The greatest message from those starlit nights is not about the depth of infinity; it is about the unlimited potential that lives within each of us. That picture of the endless heavens is a perfect metaphor for the promise and potential that each of us is born to possess. But instead of living "out there," limitless, without boundaries, we see ourselves living so stuck to our everyday life, with all of our limits, real and imagined, that we can miss the reason we came here in the first place.

When I pause long enough in life to see the starlight, and move up into it, instead of feeling insignificant, I feel empowered, capable of doing so much more than I had imagined. I reflect on the awareness that I have done so little with the time I've been given while I have been here. If I stay with it long enough, soaring freely into the stars, I begin to see the limitations of life falling away, and a core of determination within me begins to grow stronger, strengthened by the starlight and the infinite potential I have that it causes me to remember.

The idea of strength from starlight is not a new idea or whim. It is a force that has been with humankind since we were first aware enough to carve expressions of it on cavern walls for later generations to ponder, and experience for themselves.

There is something in that starlight, in those deep heavens, that I saw and recognized when I was a child, experiencing its beauty and glory for the first time. There is something there that, if we were all able to see it often in our lives, on many nights, we would think about putting our weapons away, laying down our guns, finding a new purpose, seeing our potential in a different way, and begin to create new tomorrows.

Over the years, as I moved from one place to another, I sometimes found it difficult to see those stars. It was usually the place—the city lights, the atmosphere, the clouds, the temperature—or not taking the time to do it. I found that unless you look for the stars, and go where you can see them, you can miss them entirely.

One night, during a time I was writing in an old hotel in the mountains of Arizona, I was driving very late, in the middle of the countryside, on the way to the hotel. I was thinking about what I was going to be writing the next day, when I noticed that it was a perfectly clear night. The stars were exceptionally vivid and bright.

Seeing that, and being miles from anywhere, I found an off-ramp and drove down a road that led away from the highway. When I was well away from the highway, I brought my car to a stop, turned off the lights and shut off the engine. I opened the car door, got out, shut the door, and stood beside my car in complete darkness. Except for the sky. And the sky that night was *brilliant*. Where I was, at an altitude of over six thousand feet, the starlight was so bright it caused everything to cast a shadow.

And then I looked up, and there it was—that infinite, joyous universe of stars and constellations that I had discovered with so much excitement and fear as a six-year-old kid—a deep, endless sky of stars and planets and constellations and novas and birthing stars and dying stars and infinite beginnings and endings, all happening in a time that never ends. I stood there for a long time in the cold, night air and looked at those stars.

Before I got back into my car and made my way up the highway, I looked up into the stars one final time.

Remembering the wonder and fear of the six-year-old boy I had once been, I realized I had not changed as much as I thought I had. When I looked at that universe and those stars, I was filled with the same wonder I had felt as a boy.

It was when I was a young boy that I had first thought about wanting to change the world. As I was to find, it would take a lifetime to even begin to do that. Perhaps more than one.

But it was in that starlight, and the endless mystery I found within it, that I had started my journey. And it would not be surprising to me if it was in those same stars, that my journey would take me next.

What I learned:

Starlight—deep, intense, sky-filling starlight—is the greatest teacher of both *humility* and *potential* that I have ever found. It reminds me that in that great expanse of infinity, there is a reason why each of us is here, and that there is more to each of us than we will ever know.

And it reminds me of the first words I ever wrote about life and the infinite universe, and our amazing, wonderful place within it.

You are everything that is;
Your thoughts, your life, your dreams come true.
You are everything you choose to be.
You are as unlimited as the endless universe.

Shad Helmstetter